FEARLESS
Be Courageous and Strong Through Your Faith In These Last Days

Edward D. Andrews

FEARLESS

Be Courageous and Strong Through Your Faith In These Last Days

"Fear not, for I am with you; be not dismayed, for I am your God; I will strengthen you, I will help you, I will uphold you with my righteous right hand." – Isaiah 41:10

Edward D. Andrews

Christian Publishing House

Cambridge, Ohio

Copyright © 2025 Edward D. Andrews

All rights reserved. Except for brief quotations in articles, other publications, book reviews, and blogs, no part of this book may be reproduced in any manner without prior written permission from the publishers. For information, write,

support@christianpublishers.org

FEARLESS: Be Courageous and Strong Through Your Faith In These Last Days by Edward D. Andrews

ISBN-10 : 1945757698

ISBN-13 : 978-1945757693

Table of Contents

PREFACE 7

INTRODUCTION 10

Chapter 1 – The Foundation of Fearless Faith 13

Chapter 2 – Knowing the God Who Commands Courage 20

Chapter 3 – Courage Through the Word of God....... 28

Chapter 4 – The Example of Christ's Courage........... 35

Chapter 5 – The Power of the Holy Spirit Through the Word... 43

Chapter 6 – Courage in the Midst of a Hostile World 51

Chapter 7 – The Courage of Prayerful Dependence... 59

Chapter 8 – Standing Firm Against Satan's Attacks... 65

Chapter 9 – Courage to Confess Christ Publicly 73

Chapter 10 – Courage Through Purity and Integrity 80

Chapter 11 – Courage in the Face of Death 88

Chapter 12 – Courage Through Fellowship and the Congregation 96

Chapter 13 – Fearless Leadership in the Church 104

Chapter 14 – Courage Through Suffering 112

Chapter 15 – Courage to Forgive 121

Chapter 16 – Courage in Waiting for Jehovah 128

Chapter 17 – Fearless Evangelism in a Decaying World 136

Chapter 18 – Courage in Spiritual Warfare 144

Chapter 19 – Courage in the Face of Apostasy 152

Chapter 20 – The Triumph of the Fearless 160

Appendix – Living Fearlessly in the Last Days 169

Bibliography 177

PREFACE

In every generation, the faithful have been called to live boldly amid opposition, to stand unwavering in the face of spiritual hostility, and to proclaim Jehovah's truth without compromise. The days in which we now live are marked by increasing moral collapse, doctrinal confusion, and open hostility toward biblical Christianity. Many professing believers find themselves ill-equipped to navigate the darkness, silence fear, and walk in the strength that comes only through unshakable faith. This book, *FEARLESS*, was born out of the conviction that courage is not optional for the Christian—it is commanded.

The foundation of true courage is not found in self-confidence, cultural affirmation, or emotional resilience. Rather, it is rooted entirely in the certainty of Jehovah's presence, the authority of His inspired Word, and the supreme example of Jesus Christ, who endured hostility, shame, and death in order to fulfill the divine will. The Scriptures command, "Be strong and courageous. Do not be afraid or dismayed, for Jehovah your God is with you wherever you go" (Joshua 1:9). This divine imperative is as relevant now as it was in Joshua's day.

In this volume, we will examine the many dimensions of biblical courage—its source, its expression, and its necessity in a decaying world. From the example of Christ's fearless ministry, to the spiritual armor that protects against Satan's attacks, to the power of the Holy Spirit as revealed in the

Scriptures, every chapter is designed to equip the reader with a deeper understanding of how to walk courageously in obedience. This is not a study in theoretical bravery, nor is it a motivational appeal rooted in shallow optimism. Rather, it is a thorough, Scripture-saturated exposition of what it means to be steadfast, immovable, and bold in the strength that God supplies.

This book does not offer empty platitudes, but grounded biblical instruction drawn from the inerrant Word of God. You will find no mystical emotionalism, no appeal to human psychology, and no accommodation to cultural relevance. What you will find is the unfiltered truth of Scripture applied to the real and present struggles that believers face today. The goal is not to stir fleeting feelings, but to cultivate enduring convictions that result in decisive action.

In these last days, as the love of many grows cold and apostasy increases, the need for fearless believers has never been more urgent. We must be those who confess Christ publicly, resist the devil boldly, walk in purity consistently, and preach the gospel courageously—without retreat, without apology, and without fear. The church needs leaders who will shepherd courageously, congregations who will pray dependently, and disciples who will suffer faithfully. The Scriptures are clear: the cowardly will have no part in the Kingdom (Revelation 21:8). But those who endure in faith, empowered by truth and filled with reverent fear of Jehovah, will share in the triumph of the fearless.

My prayer is that this work will be used by God to call His people back to a Scripture-rooted boldness—one that neither compromises under pressure nor yields to fear. May each reader be challenged to examine his or her life in light of God's Word, to throw off every entanglement of fear, and to run with endurance the race set before us, fixing our eyes on Jesus, the Author and Perfecter of our faith.

Edward D. Andrews

Author of 220 books and Chief Translator of the Updated American Standard Version

Edward D. Andrews

INTRODUCTION

We are living in the final stretch of a world dominated by spiritual darkness, moral decay, and escalating opposition to the truth of Scripture. The last days, as prophesied throughout both Old and New Testaments, are not merely approaching—they are upon us. From the aggressive promotion of godlessness in the public square to the internal erosion of doctrinal fidelity within professed Christian institutions, the faithful are increasingly finding themselves outnumbered, ridiculed, and pressed to compromise. The result? Many are discouraged, confused, and silent. Yet Scripture calls for none of these responses. It calls for courage—God-defined, Word-anchored, Spirit-empowered courage.

The aim of this book is to reawaken and reinforce the biblical mandate to be fearless. Not reckless. Not arrogant. But resolute and immovable. It is not enough to passively believe truth; the Christian must be willing to stand upon it when the cost is high, when the opposition is fierce, and when the consequences are severe. The Word of God does not celebrate timidity or neutrality. It calls believers to "contend earnestly for the faith that was once for all time handed down to the holy ones" (Jude 3). This requires courage—not the kind fostered by emotion or popular opinion, but the kind forged in the furnace of prayer, obedience, and unwavering trust in Jehovah.

The biblical call to fearlessness is not reserved for leaders, apostles, or prophets—it is for every man and woman who bears the name of Christ. Whether you are a father called to lead your family in righteousness, a pastor charged with feeding and protecting the flock, a student confronting the ideologies of academia, or a believer simply seeking to live godly in an ungodly world, you are called to be courageous. Jehovah never leaves this to human invention. He has provided all that is necessary for fearless living: His Word, His promises, the example of His Son, and the assurance of His abiding presence.

Joshua 1:9 declares, "Have I not commanded you? Be strong and courageous. Do not be afraid, nor be dismayed, for Jehovah your God is with you wherever you go." This verse does not suggest courage as a noble trait to be admired; it issues it as a divine command. Fearlessness is obedience. To cower when God commands boldness is to deny His sufficiency and to question His promises. When the culture rages, when the world mocks, when Satan schemes, and when even fellow Christians capitulate, the one who fears Jehovah alone will stand tall.

This book is structured to walk the believer through the biblical foundation, examples, and imperatives of godly courage. Each chapter will confront an essential dimension of fearless faith—from the foundational commands of Scripture, to the character of God who enables boldness, to the sufferings and oppositions that will inevitably come to those who are faithful. You will explore how courage is rooted in knowing God, shaped by His Word, demonstrated by

Christ, sustained in prayer, and necessary for all who would walk righteously in these closing days.

You will not find sentimental platitudes, psychological coping techniques, or worldly encouragement in these pages. You will find a return to Scripture—because only Scripture can produce real courage. You will be challenged to examine your fears, expose your compromises, and renounce the subtle ways that cowardice disguises itself as wisdom. But you will also be encouraged, emboldened, and equipped with the truth that courage is not reserved for the few. It is the inheritance of all who submit to God's Word and walk in His strength.

The goal is not temporary bravery. The goal is steadfast, enduring, God-exalting fearlessness that remains faithful until the end. The world needs fewer voices echoing compromise and more lives proclaiming, through word and deed, that truth is non-negotiable and Christ is worthy of all loyalty. The church must recover its courage—not through human effort, but by returning to the sufficiency of Scripture and the certainty of Jehovah's presence. The believer who fears God rightly fears nothing else.

You are not alone in this call. Jehovah has placed you in this generation, at this time in history, for this purpose: to be fearless for the sake of His name. May this book be a tool in His hand to awaken that resolve in your heart, and may you walk forward in faith, unshaken and immovable, as you "be courageous and strong through your faith in these last days."

Chapter 1 – The Foundation of Fearless Faith

Main Verse: "Have I not commanded you? Be strong and courageous. Do not be afraid, nor be dismayed, for Jehovah your God is with you wherever you go." — *Joshua 1:9*

The Command to Be Courageous

The call to courage in Joshua 1:9 is not merely a suggestion or encouragement; it is a divine command. Jehovah speaks directly to Joshua, not to inspire self-confidence, but to instill God-confidence. Joshua was about to lead the Israelites into Canaan after the death of Moses, a monumental task filled with formidable enemies and overwhelming challenges. The land was inhabited by nations stronger and more numerous than Israel. Yet Jehovah's words pierced through every possible fear with divine authority: "Have I not commanded you?" This phrase places courage in the context of obedience. To disobey this command would be to doubt Jehovah's faithfulness and to refuse to act upon His promises. Courage, therefore, is not an emotion one stirs up from within but a choice of will grounded in faith and obedience to God's revealed Word.

Joshua's courage was to be defined not by military strength or human wisdom but by complete reliance upon Jehovah's unfailing guidance. The courage God demands is not arrogance or recklessness but a holy boldness anchored in the certainty that His promises are true. When believers recognize that courage is a divine command, they understand that fear is not an acceptable response to the challenges of faith. Jehovah calls His people to live above fear through submission to His will and trust in His sovereignty.

Strength Rooted in Obedience

Jehovah did not tell Joshua to summon inner strength from his own heart; He directed him to find strength in obedience to His Word. In Joshua 1:7-8, Jehovah instructed, "Only be strong and very courageous, being careful to do according to all the law that Moses My servant commanded you. Do not turn from it to the right hand or to the left, that you may have good success wherever you go." This connection between strength and obedience reveals the source of spiritual fortitude. Strength does not arise from self-assurance or worldly strategy, but from faithful submission to Scripture.

When one's heart is aligned with God's commands, fear loses its grip. Obedience fosters confidence because it assures the believer of Jehovah's favor and presence. Those who walk in disobedience cannot be fearless, for they stand apart from the protective hand of God. The Word of God is the foundation of fearless faith because it reveals Jehovah's unchanging nature, His promises, and His power to accomplish His purposes through His servants.

The Christian today, like Joshua of old, is called to stand firm in obedience to the Scriptures. The world's wisdom promotes self-reliance, but the Bible declares that true strength is found in submission to the authority of Jehovah's Word. As Paul wrote, "Be strong in the Lord and in the power of His might" (Ephesians 6:10). Spiritual courage is not the absence of danger but the presence of divine strength through obedience to truth.

The Presence of Jehovah as the Source of Courage

The foundation of fearless faith is the unbreakable assurance of Jehovah's presence. In Joshua 1:9, the command to be strong and courageous rests upon the promise, "for Jehovah your God is with you wherever you go." This truth transforms fear into confidence. The believer's strength is not derived from favorable circumstances but from the abiding reality that Jehovah is ever-present.

When Moses commissioned Joshua earlier, he reminded him of this very assurance, saying, "It is Jehovah who goes before you. He will be with you; He will not leave you or forsake you. Do not fear or be dismayed" (Deuteronomy 31:8). The repetition of this promise throughout Scripture demonstrates its central importance. Fear often arises when one feels alone, but when one knows Jehovah is near, faith overcomes anxiety.

This same assurance was echoed by Jesus Christ when He told His disciples, "I am with you always, even to the end of the age" (Matthew 28:20). Jehovah's presence does not guarantee a life free from hardship, but it guarantees that no hardship will occur outside His sovereign care. The believer who walks with God never walks alone. This awareness of divine companionship provides the courage to face persecution, temptation, uncertainty, and even death with unwavering confidence.

Rejecting the Spirit of Fear

Fear is not simply a human weakness; it is a spiritual condition that arises when faith wavers. The Apostle Paul wrote to Timothy, "For God gave us not a spirit of fear, but of power and of love and of soundness of mind" (2 Timothy 1:7). The "spirit of fear" is not from God; it originates from a lack of trust in His promises and from the influence of Satan, who seeks to paralyze the believer's faith. Fear focuses on one's limitations, while faith focuses on Jehovah's unlimited power.

When believers allow fear to dominate their hearts, they deny the sufficiency of God's presence and promises. This is why the Scripture repeatedly commands, "Do not be afraid." Jehovah would not command His people to reject fear if it were not possible to do so. Through prayer, meditation on Scripture, and remembrance of Jehovah's past faithfulness, the believer can reject fear and walk in the spirit of power and love.

Courage is not the absence of fear, but the refusal to let fear rule. The Christian who trusts in Jehovah's sovereignty recognizes that fear has no rightful place in a life surrendered to God. Fear thrives in the absence of faith; faith thrives in the presence of God's truth. The believer's response to fear must therefore be rooted in the knowledge that Jehovah reigns supreme over every circumstance, and that His purposes cannot fail.

Faith That Acts in Confidence

True faith is not passive belief; it is active obedience. Joshua's courage was demonstrated by his willingness to act upon Jehovah's commands even when the outcomes seemed impossible. When he led Israel across the Jordan River and into Jericho, he did not rely on human strategy but on divine instruction. Faith that is genuine always produces obedience, for trust in God's promises leads to decisive action in accordance with His Word.

James wrote, "Faith without works is dead" (James 2:26). This does not mean that works earn salvation but that true faith expresses itself through obedience. The believer who claims to trust Jehovah yet refuses to act in accordance with His Word demonstrates unbelief. Courageous faith acts, not because the path is easy, but because God is faithful. When Israel marched around the walls of Jericho, it was not military might that brought victory but trust in the power of Jehovah.

Every believer is called to exercise this same kind of faith — faith that acts confidently in obedience to Scripture, regardless of opposition or uncertainty. The Christian must confront life's challenges with the conviction that Jehovah's promises are true and that His presence guarantees success according to His will. Fearless faith manifests in obedience that honors God even when human reason cannot comprehend the outcome.

Building an Unshakable Trust in God

Fearless faith is not built overnight; it is cultivated through continual trust in Jehovah's faithfulness. Every victory and every hardship become opportunities to deepen reliance upon Him. Just as Joshua grew in strength through each act of obedience, the believer's courage grows as he or she walks faithfully with God through all circumstances. Trust matures when the believer learns to see Jehovah's hand guiding every detail of life.

Psalm 56:3–4 declares, "When I am afraid, I put my trust in You. In God, whose word I praise — in God I trust; I shall not be afraid. What can flesh do to me?" The psalmist's words reveal the secret of unshakable trust: faith grounded in the Word of God. The more one knows Jehovah's Word, the more one knows His character, and the more one's heart rests secure in His promises.

This trust also requires humility. The proud depend on their own wisdom, but the humble place all confidence in Jehovah's direction. Proverbs 3:5–6 commands, "Trust in Jehovah with all your heart, and do not lean on your own understanding. In all your ways acknowledge Him, and He will make straight your paths." Such trust refuses to waver even when the way seems uncertain. It is in the moments of greatest uncertainty that the believer's faith shines brightest, revealing a heart anchored in divine assurance rather than worldly security.

Fearless faith is ultimately founded upon the character of God Himself. Because Jehovah is unchanging, His people can be unshakable. Because He is faithful, they can be fearless. Because He is sovereign, they can be strong and courageous. The Christian who builds life upon this foundation will find that no storm can destroy what God has established. Courage flows naturally from the conviction that Jehovah's promises never fail and that His presence never departs.

Edward D. Andrews

Chapter 2 – Knowing the God Who Commands Courage

Main Verse: "The people who know their God will be strong and take action." — Daniel 11:32

The Nature and Attributes of Jehovah

To truly understand the courage and strength that come from knowing God, we must first grasp who Jehovah is in His revealed nature and attributes. Jehovah is the eternal, self-existent One, whose personal name conveys the meaning "He Causes to Become." This emphasizes His active role in fulfilling His purposes and promises throughout human history. He is omnipotent, omniscient, and omnipresent—yet also righteous, loving, and just. His holiness separates Him from all imperfection, and His love motivates all that He does for the redemption and restoration of humanity.

Jehovah's power is not arbitrary but moral and purposeful. His might sustains creation, but His holiness governs His every act. Unlike the false gods of the nations, Jehovah is not a projection of human imagination; He is the living and personal God who reveals Himself through His Word and His works. Scripture reveals that Jehovah is "slow to anger and abundant in loyal love and truth" (Exodus 34:6). He does not change (Malachi 3:6), nor does He grow weary (Isaiah 40:28). His consistency and moral perfection make Him utterly reliable, a foundation of stability for those who trust Him.

To know Jehovah, therefore, is not merely to recognize His existence but to enter into a covenantal understanding of His revealed person—His moral attributes, His faithfulness to His promises, and His sovereignty over all creation. Courage arises not from our own confidence but from this unshakable assurance that Jehovah's power and wisdom are always directed by His righteousness and love.

Knowing God Versus Knowing About Him

There is a vast difference between knowing about God and truly knowing Him. Many people possess information about Jehovah from Scripture or tradition, yet they have not entered into the relational knowledge that transforms character and fuels faithfulness. Knowing God in the biblical sense involves intimate fellowship and obedient faith. The Hebrew word *yada'*, translated "know," often implies relational closeness and experiential understanding rather than intellectual awareness.

Daniel 11:32 draws a sharp distinction between those who merely profess faith and those who truly know their God. The historical context of Daniel's prophecy reveals a time of persecution, deception, and compromise. Yet, in the midst of apostasy, a remnant would "know their God," and this knowledge would empower them to "be strong and take action." It is not theological sophistication that produces courage, but genuine acquaintance with the living God.

This kind of knowledge is cultivated through the study of His Word and the practice of prayerful obedience. As the psalmist declared, "Those who know Your name will trust in You, for You, O Jehovah, have not abandoned those who seek You" (Psalm 9:10). The more we know His name—His revealed character—the more steadfast our trust becomes. Knowing about God fills the mind, but knowing God transforms the heart. One may recite facts about His attributes yet remain unchanged; only through submission and reverence does knowledge become the strength that resists fear and compromise.

The Strength That Comes from Intimacy with God

When Daniel prophesied that those who know their God would "be strong," he referred not to natural courage or self-confidence but to divine empowerment that results from intimate fellowship with Jehovah. This strength is moral and spiritual rather than physical, sustained by conviction that rests on God's immutable promises.

Throughout Scripture, strength and courage are always linked to God's presence and Word. When Jehovah commissioned Joshua to lead Israel into Canaan, He commanded, "Be strong and courageous. Do not be terrified, nor be dismayed, for Jehovah your God is with you wherever you go" (Joshua 1:9). The foundation of courage was not Joshua's leadership ability or Israel's numbers, but Jehovah's companionship and faithfulness to His Word. The same is true for all who trust in Him today.

Spiritual strength comes when faith clings to Jehovah's revealed truth even when circumstances appear overwhelming. The psalmist wrote, "Jehovah is my light and my salvation; whom should I fear? Jehovah is the stronghold of my life; of whom should I be afraid?" (Psalm 27:1). Fear fades where the presence of God is recognized. When believers cultivate intimacy with Him through study, meditation, and obedience, courage becomes the natural fruit of their relationship. They do not rely on fluctuating emotions but on the steadfast character of Jehovah, who never fails.

This intimacy also transforms how we face adversity. Those who know God personally do not interpret suffering as abandonment but as an opportunity to prove His faithfulness. They recall His past deliverances and promises, drawing renewed strength from His unchanging nature.

Thus, the knowledge of God does not exempt His people from hardship but equips them to endure it victoriously.

Obedience as the Expression of Knowing Him

Obedience is not the pathway to knowing God—it is the inevitable expression of truly knowing Him. When a believer perceives Jehovah's holiness and majesty, the only fitting response is submission. "By this we know that we have come to know Him, if we keep His commandments" (1 John 2:3). Genuine knowledge of God is inseparable from conformity to His will.

The command to "be strong and take action" in Daniel 11:32 does not suggest reckless zeal but deliberate obedience. The Hebrew phrase implies standing firm and doing great exploits—acts of faithfulness rooted in conviction. This courage flows from the confidence that obedience to Jehovah's Word is always right, regardless of opposition.

History bears witness to men and women who displayed this kind of courage because they knew God. Moses stood before Pharaoh because he trusted in Jehovah's deliverance. David faced Goliath not with bravado but with faith in the living God. Daniel himself defied decrees that forbade prayer, because he valued obedience to Jehovah above personal safety. In each case, courage was the visible manifestation of inward devotion.

Those who truly know Jehovah find that obedience becomes their delight rather than their burden. His commandments are not grievous, for they reflect His own righteous character. Obedience then becomes a declaration of love and trust. As Jesus said, "If anyone loves Me, he will keep My word, and My Father will love him, and We will come to him and make Our dwelling with him" (John 14:23). To know God is to walk in His ways; to walk in His ways is to display courage in a hostile world.

The Fear of Jehovah as the Beginning of Wisdom

True knowledge of God begins with reverential fear. "The fear of Jehovah is the beginning of wisdom, and the knowledge of the Holy One is insight" (Proverbs 9:10). This fear is not terror of punishment but deep respect for His authority, holiness, and justice. It is a moral awareness of God's greatness that produces humility and obedience.

Without the fear of Jehovah, courage degenerates into arrogance. The fear of Jehovah purifies motives and anchors faith. It teaches us that courage is not defiance of authority but alignment with divine truth. When believers fear Jehovah rightly, they fear nothing else. This was the secret of Daniel's steadfastness in Babylon. Though surrounded by idolatry and political intimidation, he feared Jehovah more than men. His reverence produced unyielding courage.

Wisdom begins when we recognize Jehovah's rightful dominion over every sphere of life. His commandments define righteousness; His purposes determine destiny. To fear Him is to acknowledge His sovereignty and to conform to His will. Such fear dispels anxiety, for we know that all things are under His control. It was this reverential awe that empowered the prophets, apostles, and faithful ones throughout Scripture to act with unshakable resolve.

Therefore, courage and wisdom grow together. As we deepen in our understanding of Jehovah's majesty, we act more decisively for His glory. The fear of Jehovah is not a hindrance to strength—it is its foundation. Those who revere Him walk securely, for they know that He upholds the righteous and frustrates the plans of the wicked.

Standing Firm Because We Know His Character

In times of moral decline, persecution, and uncertainty, the people who know their God stand firm because they understand His character. They have learned through Scripture and experience that Jehovah is faithful to every promise, just in every judgment, and loving in every discipline. They do not measure His goodness by their comfort but by His revealed Word.

Standing firm does not mean mere resistance; it means active loyalty to Jehovah in thought, word, and deed. The early Christians who faced opposition from Rome did not yield because they knew the risen Christ and trusted His promise of resurrection. Their courage was not born of rebellion but of faith. Likewise, modern believers who know Jehovah's truth are called to stand unmoved amid the shifting values of a corrupt world.

When Daniel foresaw that "the people who know their God will be strong and take action," he described more than mere human perseverance; he foretold the triumph of faith that refuses compromise. Those who know Jehovah do not need to search for courage—it flows naturally from the conviction that He reigns supreme. They remember His deliverance of Israel, His faithfulness to His covenant, His victory in Christ, and His coming Kingdom.

Knowing God transforms fear into faith, hesitation into obedience, and weakness into endurance. Every act of courage in Scripture arose from confidence in God's unchanging character. Therefore, the call to "be strong and take action" is, at its heart, a call to intimacy with the living God. The more deeply we know Him, the more steadfastly we stand, for His strength becomes our own.

Chapter 3 – Courage Through the Word of God

Main Verse: "Your word is a lamp to my feet and a light to my path." — Psalm 119:105

The Word as the Source of Spiritual Strength

True courage in the Christian life does not come from personal confidence, human strength, or emotional resilience. It arises from a deep and abiding trust in Jehovah through His inspired Word. The psalmist declared that God's Word is "a lamp to my feet and a light to my path" (Psalm 119:105), signifying that divine revelation is the believer's sole guide through the darkness of this fallen world. The Scriptures illuminate the path of righteousness, exposing the snares of sin and the deceitful schemes of Satan. The Word of God does not merely inform—it transforms, producing within the believer a steadfast courage to stand firm amid adversity.

Jehovah's Word provides strength that transcends human frailty. When Joshua was called to lead Israel after Moses' death, Jehovah did not give him a strategy of warfare or worldly leadership principles but commanded, "Be strong and very courageous. Be careful to do according to all the law that Moses my servant commanded you; do not turn from it to the right or to the left, that you may have success wherever you go. This book of the law shall not depart from your mouth, but you shall meditate on it day and night" (Joshua 1:7–8). Courage, therefore, is inseparable from obedience to Scripture. The believer who draws his strength from the Word will not collapse under pressure, for his courage is anchored in the unchanging promises of Jehovah.

Spiritual courage comes when the heart is fortified by truth. Every great act of faith in biblical history was preceded by confidence in the veracity of God's Word. Abraham left Ur because Jehovah's Word assured him of a covenant promise. David confronted Goliath because he trusted the God who had already delivered him from the lion and the bear. Daniel faced the lions' den because he held fast to the authority of the Word of God above the decrees of kings. The Word builds within the believer a courage not based on external success or visible outcomes but on the conviction that Jehovah's Word cannot fail.

Scripture's Power to Remove Fear and Doubt

Fear and doubt are the natural responses of the fallen human heart, but Jehovah's Word uproots both by revealing His sovereignty and faithfulness. When the believer fills his mind with Scripture, he learns to see circumstances through the lens of divine truth rather than human perception. Isaiah wrote, "You will keep him in perfect peace, whose mind is stayed on you, because he trusts in you" (Isaiah 26:3). That peace is the product of meditating upon the truth of God's Word until fear is driven away.

The apostle Paul instructed Timothy that "God gave us not a spirit of fear, but of power and love and self-control" (2 Timothy 1:7). That spirit of power is not some mystical force; it is the strength that flows from understanding and applying Scripture. When Christ's words dwell richly in the heart, fear loses its dominion. Jesus Himself demonstrated this when confronting temptation in the wilderness. He countered every satanic deception with the Word of God, declaring, "It is written" (Matthew 4:4, 7, 10). This reveals that Scripture, when believed and spoken, disarms the lies that produce fear and doubt.

The psalmist experienced this same reality: "When I am afraid, I put my trust in you. In God, whose word I praise, in God I trust; I shall not be afraid" (Psalm 56:3–4). Trust in Jehovah's Word dispels fear because it centers the believer's heart upon the absolute reliability of God's promises. Fear thrives in ignorance of the Word, but faith thrives in its illumination. To remove fear, one must not seek comfort in fleeting emotions but in the objective truth of Scripture.

The Authority and Sufficiency of the Word

The believer's courage is sustained only when he recognizes the complete authority and sufficiency of God's Word. Scripture is not a mere source of encouragement; it is the final and infallible revelation of Jehovah's will. As Paul wrote, "All Scripture is inspired by God and beneficial for teaching, for reproving, for setting things straight, for disciplining in righteousness, that the man of God may be complete, equipped for every good work" (2 Timothy 3:16–17). The courage to stand in a morally decaying world comes from knowing that the Bible is entirely trustworthy, inerrant, and sufficient for every matter of faith and life.

The authority of Scripture gives the believer the moral confidence to resist the tide of compromise. Courage is not mere boldness—it is the strength to stand firm in obedience when others yield to error. The prophet Jeremiah is an example of this kind of courage. Despite facing opposition from kings, priests, and false prophets, he proclaimed Jehovah's Word without alteration. He could do so because he knew that the message he carried came from the mouth of God. Likewise, the Christian must hold fast to the authority of Scripture in a world that increasingly denies absolute truth.

The sufficiency of the Word assures the believer that he lacks nothing for a godly and courageous life. Many today seek courage through motivational teachings, emotional experiences, or worldly philosophy, but only Scripture provides the lasting foundation for spiritual boldness. The Word of God is "living and active, sharper than any two-edged sword" (Hebrews 4:12). It pierces the heart, renews the mind, and produces endurance through trials. The believer who fully submits to its authority and sufficiency stands unshaken amid persecution and uncertainty.

Meditating on God's Word Daily

Courage is not sustained by occasional contact with Scripture but by daily meditation upon it. The psalmist wrote, "Blessed is the man who walks not in the counsel of the wicked... but his delight is in the law of Jehovah, and on his law he meditates day and night" (Psalm 1:1–2). Meditation here is not a mystical practice but a deliberate pondering and internalizing of God's Word until it governs one's thoughts and actions.

Daily meditation strengthens spiritual discernment. When the believer continually fills his heart with divine truth, he learns to interpret life according to Jehovah's wisdom rather than human reasoning. This produces a quiet yet immovable courage, because every decision, every reaction, and every hope is anchored in the Word. Meditation also transforms fear into faith, as continual reflection upon God's promises trains the heart to trust in His unchanging nature.

This discipline was exemplified by Jesus Christ Himself. During His earthly ministry, He often withdrew to solitary places to commune with the Father through prayer and reflection upon Scripture. His courage in facing rejection, betrayal, and the cross was not a result of human determination but of perfect submission to the Father's will as revealed in the Word. In imitation of Christ, the believer must cultivate the habit of daily meditation, letting Scripture become the constant source of courage and guidance.

Faith Comes by Hearing the Word of Christ

The apostle Paul wrote, "So faith comes from hearing, and hearing through the word of Christ" (Romans 10:17). Faith—and thus courage—cannot exist apart from the message of Scripture. The Word produces faith because it reveals the character and promises of Jehovah. Each time the believer reads or hears Scripture, the Spirit-energized Word strengthens conviction and builds endurance.

Courage is the visible expression of faith. When one believes God's promises as absolute truth, he acts upon them without hesitation, even when the world mocks or threatens. The heroes of faith in Hebrews 11 were not superhuman; they were men and women whose faith was founded upon God's Word. They "considered Him faithful who had promised" (Hebrews 11:11), and their courage flowed from that conviction.

Hearing the Word continually renews courage because it refocuses the mind upon divine reality rather than worldly fear. The more the believer exposes himself to Scripture, the more his thoughts, emotions, and responses align with God's will. When trials arise, courage flows naturally from a heart saturated with the Word of Christ.

Using Scripture as the Sword Against Fear

The believer's courage is not passive; it is an active defense and offense against fear. Paul described the Word of God as "the sword of the Spirit" (Ephesians 6:17), the only offensive weapon in the armor of God. This imagery shows that courage is not achieved through human willpower but through wielding the truth of Scripture against the lies of fear.

Every fear originates in deception—whether about God's power, His goodness, or His control. Scripture exposes these falsehoods and replaces them with truth. When Satan tempted Christ with doubt and fear, Jesus answered decisively with the written Word. The believer must do the same, responding to fear not with self-reliance but with Scripture that affirms Jehovah's sovereignty and love.

The sword of the Spirit must be used skillfully. This requires more than memorization; it requires comprehension, meditation, and application. A soldier who neglects his weapon in peace will be unprepared in battle. Likewise, a Christian who neglects the study of Scripture will falter when fear strikes. Courage is forged in the quiet moments of study, prayer, and obedience, long before the crisis comes.

When the believer meets fear with the Word, fear retreats. The truth of Scripture pierces the darkness of uncertainty and anchors the soul in the faithfulness of God. Thus, courage through the Word of God is not a momentary feeling but a continual stance of trust, grounded in divine revelation.

Chapter 4 – The Example of Christ's Courage

Main Verse: "Who for the joy that was set before him endured the cross, despising the shame." — *Hebrews 12:2*

The Boldness of Jesus Before Men

The courage of Jesus Christ stands as the supreme model of fearless devotion to Jehovah's purpose and will. From the beginning of His ministry, Jesus displayed an unwavering boldness in declaring the truth, regardless of the opposition He faced. He was not intimidated by the religious establishment of His day, nor did He seek human approval. His words were filled with divine authority and spiritual power. When He entered the synagogues, He taught not as the scribes but as One bearing the authority of Jehovah Himself (Mark 1:22). His boldness was not rooted in human pride but in His perfect confidence in His Father's will.

When confronted by the Pharisees and Sadducees—men who prided themselves on their knowledge of the Law—Jesus exposed their hypocrisy without hesitation. He declared, "Woe to you, scribes and Pharisees, hypocrites! For you shut the kingdom of heaven in people's faces" (Matthew 23:13). These words reflected divine courage, for He spoke them in a setting where rejection, ridicule, and eventual violence were guaranteed. Yet, His boldness was inseparable from His love. His courage was not reckless or vengeful; it was the courageous love of truth that refused to compromise or flatter. He loved righteousness and hated wickedness (Hebrews 1:9). His mission required that He confront sin openly and call men to repentance, knowing that this would ultimately lead to His suffering and death.

The courage of Jesus before men teaches that faithfulness to Jehovah demands fearless proclamation of truth. True courage in God's service is not measured by outward aggression or worldly confidence, but by quiet, unwavering faith in God's Word and purpose, even when the cost is personal loss, social rejection, or death itself.

Courage in the Face of Rejection and Suffering

From His hometown of Nazareth, where His own neighbors rejected Him, to Jerusalem, where the leaders plotted His death, Jesus endured rejection with calm resolve. When the people of Nazareth sought to throw Him off a cliff after His first public reading of Isaiah 61 (Luke 4:28–30), He did not retaliate or flee in fear. He simply walked through their midst, demonstrating that no human power could thwart the divine timetable for His ministry. His composure under threat was a reflection of His unbroken trust in Jehovah's protection and plan.

Throughout His ministry, Jesus faced constant opposition—misrepresentation, false accusation, and persecution. Yet He did not allow bitterness to take root. When He was falsely accused of being a drunkard, a blasphemer, and even possessed by demons, He calmly continued His mission. When His disciples deserted Him, He did not despair. When He was betrayed by Judas and denied by Peter, He remained steadfast, fulfilling His Father's will. His courage was not dependent on human support but on the assurance that His Father's purpose could not fail.

This courage shines most clearly in Gethsemane, where the pressure of the coming suffering pressed so deeply upon Him that His sweat became like drops of blood. Yet in that hour, Jesus prayed, "My Father, if this cannot pass unless I drink it, your will be done" (Matthew 26:42). Courage is not the absence of distress but the mastery of it through faith. Jesus' submission to His Father's will, even in the face of death, demonstrates the essence of divine courage.

Edward D. Andrews

The Cross as the Ultimate Expression of Fearless Faith

The cross of Christ stands as the highest demonstration of fearless faith. He knew the manner of death awaiting Him long before it came. He foretold to His disciples, "The Son of Man must suffer many things ... and be killed, and on the third day be raised" (Luke 9:22). Knowing this, He continued steadfastly toward Jerusalem (Luke 9:51). Every step toward the cross was a step of deliberate obedience, not resignation. The Gospels describe His demeanor before Pilate and the Roman soldiers as calm and controlled. When falsely accused, He did not answer in self-defense, fulfilling Isaiah's prophecy: "He was oppressed, and He was afflicted, yet He opened not His mouth" (Isaiah 53:7).

On the cross, He endured not only physical agony but the moral and spiritual weight of bearing the world's sin. The shame of crucifixion—public humiliation, nakedness, and mockery—was something He despised, yet He accepted it for the joy set before Him: the joy of accomplishing redemption and glorifying His Father. His endurance was not passive suffering but active, victorious faith. The joy that sustained Him was the certainty of resurrection, the vindication of Jehovah's righteousness, and the salvation of obedient mankind.

The cross, therefore, is the ultimate expression of courageous love. Jesus faced what no human before or after could endure. His courage was not only moral but spiritual; He stood alone against the full force of human sin, Satanic hatred, and divine justice. His cry, "It is finished!" (John 19:30), was not a cry of defeat but the triumphant declaration of completed obedience.

Christ's Confidence in His Father's Will

The courage of Christ was inseparably linked to His confidence in His Father. He knew that His Father's wisdom and justice were perfect, and therefore, He never questioned the righteousness of the path laid before Him. He declared, "My food is to do the will of him who sent me and to accomplish his work" (John 4:34). His confidence was founded on absolute trust that Jehovah's promises would be fulfilled.

Even as the shadow of the cross fell over Him, He could say, "Now is my soul troubled. And what shall I say? 'Father, save me from this hour'? But for this purpose I have come to this hour. Father, glorify your name" (John 12:27–28). His courage did not rest upon self-sufficiency but upon surrender to divine authority. He was fearless because He was faithful, and His faithfulness was grounded in His perfect knowledge of His Father's goodness.

In every stage of His life, Jesus entrusted Himself to the One who judges righteously (1 Peter 2:23). This confidence enabled Him to endure betrayal, mockery, scourging, and crucifixion without losing composure or love. His courage, therefore, was not stoic indifference but serene trust. He endured not because He was insensible to pain, but because His will was completely aligned with His Father's.

Following the Path of Obedient Endurance

Christ's example calls His followers to a life of obedient endurance. The writer of Hebrews commands believers to "consider him who endured from sinners such hostility against himself, so that you may not grow weary or fainthearted" (Hebrews 12:3). The courage of Christ is not merely an object of admiration but a pattern to be imitated. Christians are called to take up their own cross daily (Luke 9:23), meaning that they must be willing to endure suffering, rejection, or loss for the sake of truth and righteousness.

Obedient endurance does not mean blind submission but steadfast adherence to Jehovah's Word despite difficulty. When believers fix their eyes on Jesus, the pioneer and perfecter of faith, they find strength to resist the pressures of this world. The early Christians understood this principle well. Facing persecution from the Roman Empire, they drew courage from Christ's example. Their faithfulness was sustained by the same joy that strengthened their Lord—the joy of eternal life and the vindication of Jehovah's name.

The believer's courage, like Christ's, is rooted in trust. When one's confidence is in human wisdom or material security, courage collapses under strain. But when faith is anchored in God's promises, endurance becomes possible. The Christian's hope is not based on immediate relief or worldly approval, but on the certainty that Jehovah's purpose will be fulfilled through Christ's Kingdom. Therefore, courage in the Christian life is not a transient emotion but a settled conviction that obedience to God's Word is worth any cost.

Courage Through Imitation of the Master

To imitate Christ's courage is to follow His example of faith, humility, and obedience. Courage is not an innate human trait; it is a spiritual discipline that grows through prayer, study of Scripture, and reliance on Jehovah's strength. Jesus' courage was sustained through constant communion with His Father. He often withdrew to solitary places to pray (Luke 5:16), demonstrating that true strength comes from dependence upon God, not independence from Him.

Believers today face a world that increasingly despises the truth of Scripture. The moral and spiritual corruption of modern society demands courage to speak and live according to God's standards. This courage must reflect the spirit of Christ—firm yet gentle, bold yet compassionate. Christians must not fear ridicule, rejection, or persecution, for they know that their reward is with Jehovah. As Jesus said, "Blessed are those who are persecuted for righteousness' sake, for theirs is the kingdom of heaven" (Matthew 5:10).

Imitating the courage of Christ involves more than enduring suffering; it involves bearing witness to the truth in love. It means confronting falsehood, hypocrisy, and sin, not with arrogance but with conviction. It means forgiving those who wrong us, as Jesus forgave His executioners, saying,

"Father, forgive them, for they know not what they do" (Luke 23:34). Such courage reveals the transforming power of divine grace.

Therefore, every follower of Christ must strive to reflect His courage by standing firm in faith, persevering under pressure, and maintaining loyalty to Jehovah's Word. The Christian's confidence, like Christ's, is anchored in the joy set before them—the hope of eternal life on a restored earth under Christ's righteous rule. The courage of Jesus is the pattern of victorious endurance, and those who follow Him in this path will share in His triumph.

Chapter 5 – The Power of the Holy Spirit Through the Word

Main Verse: "For God gave us not a spirit of fear, but of power and love and soundness of mind." — 2 Timothy 1:7

The Role of the Spirit Through the Scriptures

The Holy Spirit is the active force of Jehovah, operating through His inspired Word to accomplish divine purposes in the lives of those who love Him. The Scriptures never describe the Spirit as an impersonal energy nor as an indwelling mystical presence, but rather as the personal power and influence of God Himself. Through the Word, the Spirit directs, convicts, strengthens, and enlightens the faithful.

Jehovah has always accomplished His will through His Spirit—whether in creation (Genesis 1:2), prophecy (2 Peter 1:21), or the giving of Scripture (2 Timothy 3:16).

When Paul wrote to Timothy, he reminded him that the gift God provided was not one that produces fear or cowardice, but rather a spirit characterized by power, love, and soundness of mind. This power is not emotional excitement nor an inward mystical experience; it is the spiritual fortitude and wisdom that come through the Word of God. Timothy's courage and stability in ministry were not to arise from his own strength, but from the truth and authority revealed through the Scriptures. The Spirit does not impart new revelations today, nor does He dwell within believers in a personal sense. Instead, He operates through the inspired Word that He caused to be written, guiding believers as they study, understand, and apply it.

The Holy Spirit was the divine agent by which the Scriptures came into being, ensuring that the words recorded were the very thoughts of God expressed through chosen men. As Paul wrote, "All Scripture is inspired of God and beneficial for teaching, for reproving, for setting things straight, for disciplining in righteousness" (2 Timothy 3:16). The power of the Spirit is therefore inseparable from the power of the Word. The same Spirit who inspired the Bible continues to work through it, bringing about faith, transformation, and endurance in those who receive it with a humble and obedient heart.

Power Rooted in the Truth of the Word

Spiritual power is not measured by emotion or by outward demonstration but by steadfast adherence to the truth. The believer's strength is found not in self-reliance, but in reliance upon the Spirit-inspired Word. When Jesus faced Satan's temptations in the wilderness, He overcame not by divine privilege, but by the power of Scripture, responding, "It is written" (Matthew 4:4, 7, 10). His example illustrates that the power of the Spirit always operates in harmony with the written Word.

This power transforms the mind (Romans 12:2) and equips the believer to live in holiness and truth. It is not a force that overrides human will, but one that enlightens the understanding and strengthens conviction. Through diligent study and meditation on Scripture, the Christian becomes empowered to resist falsehood, overcome fear, and display love and self-control. The Word does not simply inform the believer; it reforms the inner life, aligning it with the will of Jehovah.

The early disciples experienced the Spirit's power through their obedience to the Word. They were emboldened to proclaim the gospel even amid persecution because they were convinced of the truth revealed to them. The same power continues today through the same Word, working in the hearts of those who submit to its authority. The Spirit's strength is manifested in patient endurance, courage under opposition, and unwavering faith in God's promises.

The Spirit's Guidance Through Illumination

The Spirit's role in the believer's life is to illuminate, not to inspire new revelation. The canon of Scripture is complete; nothing is to be added or removed (Revelation 22:18–19). However, through illumination, the Spirit enables the humble reader to discern the meaning and application of divine truth. This illumination is not mystical or emotional but rational and moral. It involves the opening of the understanding through the power of God's Word itself, allowing the believer to grasp the intent of Scripture and to be molded by it.

Jesus promised that the Spirit would "guide you into all the truth" (John 16:13). This guidance was fulfilled initially in the apostles, who were inspired to record the divine message accurately. Today, the Spirit continues to guide through the completed Word, making its message clear to those who approach it with reverence and faith. This illumination does not bypass reason or study; rather, it demands diligent effort, as the believer rightly divides the Word of truth (2 Timothy 2:15). The Spirit does not reveal truth apart from Scripture but through it, applying its message to the mind and conscience of the faithful.

A Christian who studies with prayerful dependence upon God's Word experiences this illumination. As the Scriptures are read and understood, the Spirit empowers discernment, enabling the believer to distinguish between truth and error. Thus, the believer grows in maturity and stability, equipped for every good work. The Spirit's power through illumination brings unity of mind, moral clarity, and strength of conviction in a world darkened by confusion.

Sound Judgment in an Age of Confusion

Paul's phrase "soundness of mind" in 2 Timothy 1:7 points to self-discipline, wisdom, and spiritual balance. The Spirit, operating through the Word, grants the believer the ability to think clearly and act wisely according to divine principles. In an age filled with emotionalism, false prophecy, and doctrinal distortion, the Spirit's work through Scripture provides the only sure foundation for judgment and stability.

Soundness of mind is not the absence of emotion, but the presence of order. The Word of God trains the mind to think biblically, to weigh decisions according to eternal truth rather than cultural pressure. The believer who yields to the teaching of Scripture becomes grounded, stable, and discerning. This balance is the result of divine truth shaping human thought.

The Holy Spirit never contradicts what He has revealed in Scripture. Therefore, any claim of the Spirit's "leading" that departs from biblical teaching must be rejected. Sound judgment is maintained only when the believer submits to the written Word as the sole rule of faith and practice. The Spirit does not give new prophecies, emotional impulses, or mystical impressions. He strengthens the believer through the timeless truths already recorded.

This balance of power, love, and soundness of mind guards the Christian from fanaticism on one side and fearfulness on the other. Through Scripture, the Spirit produces courage tempered by wisdom, zeal guided by knowledge, and love strengthened by truth.

Courage Empowered by Divine Truth

The Spirit's power through the Word emboldens the believer to stand firm in the face of opposition. Courage does not arise from self-confidence, but from confidence in God's revealed truth. Timothy faced persecution, false teachers, and hostility from a corrupt world. Yet Paul reminded him that God had already provided the necessary strength through the Spirit. The same is true for every Christian today.

Courage grounded in Scripture is fearless because it is faith-based. The believer knows that Jehovah's Word cannot fail. When Elijah confronted the prophets of Baal, his confidence was not in himself but in the Word and power of God. When Daniel refused to bow to idolatry, his resolve came from a heart strengthened by divine truth. When the apostles faced imprisonment, their courage flowed from their conviction that the risen Christ was guiding them through His Spirit and Word.

This courage is not reckless; it is reasoned and disciplined. The Spirit produces love and sound judgment alongside power, ensuring that boldness does not become arrogance. The courage born of the Spirit is compassionate, wise, and steadfast. It refuses to compromise truth for acceptance, and it endures hardship with faith that Jehovah's purposes will prevail.

Standing Strong in Spirit-Filled Understanding

To stand strong in a world hostile to divine truth requires the full measure of the Spirit's influence through Scripture. The believer must be anchored in the Word, trained by its instruction, and molded by its wisdom. The Spirit's power works not by bypassing the intellect, but by renewing it. Through constant meditation on the Scriptures, the mind is fortified, and the heart is strengthened.

Spirit-filled understanding is characterized by humility, obedience, and love for truth. It is not a special emotional state but a mature comprehension of God's revealed will. Those who are filled with the Word are filled with the Spirit, for the two are inseparable. The Spirit's influence transforms thinking, shapes conduct, and produces spiritual fruit. This is why Paul exhorted believers to "be filled with the Spirit" (Ephesians 5:18) and to "let the word of Christ dwell in you richly" (Colossians 3:16). These parallel commands show that the Spirit's filling occurs through the internalization of Scripture.

The Christian who walks in this Spirit-filled understanding is unmoved by fear or falsehood. His faith is not shaken by shifting philosophies or worldly pressures, because his confidence rests upon the eternal Word. The

Spirit's power through Scripture equips the believer to overcome sin, to discern truth from error, to love sincerely, and to endure faithfully until the end.

In every generation, the same Spirit who inspired the Scriptures continues to work through them, calling men and women to faith, equipping them for righteousness, and empowering them to live in courage, love, and sound judgment. Those who rely on this divine power stand firm, not through human strength, but through the living Word that reveals the mind and will of Jehovah.

Chapter 6 – Courage in the Midst of a Hostile World

Main Verse: "If the world hates you, you know that it has hated me before it hated you." — John 15:18

Understanding the World's Hostility

The words of Jesus in John 15:18 penetrate the heart of every sincere believer living in a fallen world. He did not hide from His followers the truth that discipleship comes with opposition. The term "world" (Greek *kosmos*) in this passage does not refer to the physical earth or humanity in general but to the organized system of human society alienated from God, ruled by Satan, and governed by principles contrary to divine truth. Jesus described this *world* as being under "the ruler of this world" (John 12:31; 14:30), referring to Satan, whose influence pervades its culture, morality, and priorities.

From the beginning, hostility toward those who belong to Jehovah has been a defining characteristic of the world's system. Abel was murdered by Cain because his works were righteous (Genesis 4:8; 1 John 3:12). The prophets were persecuted because they spoke Jehovah's words without compromise (Matthew 5:12). The world's hatred is not merely emotional; it is spiritual rebellion. Jesus Christ is the perfect embodiment of truth, holiness, and love, and the world that is enslaved to darkness reacts violently against His light (John 3:19-20).

Christ's warning was not intended to discourage His followers but to prepare them. The Christian must understand that persecution is not evidence of failure but confirmation of loyalty to Christ. The world's hostility validates the believer's separation from its values and its ruler. To love God's truth necessarily provokes the hatred of those who reject it.

The Reality of Spiritual Opposition

The believer's conflict is not ultimately with flesh and blood but with spiritual forces of wickedness in the heavenly realms (Ephesians 6:12). Satan, the adversary, manipulates human systems, philosophies, and institutions to oppose the Kingdom of God. His goal is to intimidate believers into silence, compromise, or apostasy. The apostle Peter warned, "Your adversary, the devil, walks about like a roaring lion, seeking someone to devour" (1 Peter 5:8). Yet Peter also commanded believers to "resist him, firm in the faith" (1 Peter 5:9).

Spiritual opposition manifests itself in various ways. It may appear as open persecution, governmental oppression, cultural mockery, or intellectual ridicule. At times, it arises subtly through worldly pleasures and ideologies designed to draw Christians into conformity. The devil's hostility is relentless, yet his power is limited by Jehovah's sovereign authority. The Christian must remember that Satan was defeated at the cross (John 12:31; Colossians 2:15). The decisive victory belongs to Christ, though the battle continues until His return.

Every generation of believers must contend for the faith once delivered to the holy ones (Jude 3). The early disciples faced imprisonment, torture, and death. Today, the conflict persists through different means—social hostility, moral pressure, and the elevation of human opinion above Scripture. Yet the source remains the same: enmity toward the authority and truth of Jehovah. Courage, therefore, is not optional but essential for those who walk with Christ.

Loving Truth in an Age That Despises It

In a world that celebrates relativism and moral ambiguity, the Christian's commitment to absolute truth is viewed as narrow and intolerant. Yet truth is not an abstract idea but the very character of God revealed in His Word. Jesus declared, "Your word is truth" (John 17:17). To love truth is to love Jehovah Himself, for He is "the God of truth" (Deuteronomy 32:4).

Loving truth in a hostile world requires both conviction and compassion. It means standing firm on the authority of Scripture even when society redefines morality, gender, or the value of life. The faithful Christian does not conform to cultural trends but transforms his mind through the Word of God (Romans 12:2). Truth is not negotiable; it is eternal. When the believer proclaims Christ as "the way and the truth and the life" (John 14:6), he challenges the world's pluralism and self-sufficiency.

The love of truth also produces spiritual discernment. The Apostle John wrote, "Do not love the world or the things in the world" (1 John 2:15). The believer who loves the truth will reject worldly philosophies that deny the authority of Scripture or undermine the sufficiency of Christ. In an age where deception flourishes, discernment preserves the believer's mind from corruption and compromise.

Loving truth demands that the Christian speak with grace but without apology. Jesus did not conceal His message to avoid offending His hearers. He spoke with divine authority, revealing the sinfulness of man and the necessity of repentance. To follow Him means proclaiming His message with the same clarity, trusting that the Spirit-inspired Word will accomplish Jehovah's purpose (Isaiah 55:11).

Maintaining Faith Under Pressure

Faithfulness in a hostile world is the measure of true discipleship. Jesus said, "He who endures to the end will be saved" (Matthew 24:13). The believer's endurance is not passive resignation but active perseverance grounded in faith. When external pressure mounts—whether through persecution, rejection, or hardship—the Christian must rely on the promises of God rather than human strength.

Hebrews 11 records the endurance of faithful men and women who remained steadfast amid severe opposition. They were mocked, imprisoned, and killed, yet they maintained their trust in Jehovah's promises. Their faith was not contingent upon favorable circumstances but upon the certainty of God's Word. Similarly, the believer today must view trials through the lens of eternity. Temporary suffering cannot compare to the glory that will be revealed in those who remain loyal to Christ (Romans 8:18).

Maintaining faith requires a life anchored in prayer, study of Scripture, and fellowship with other believers. Isolation weakens courage, but unity strengthens it. Christians draw courage from the assurance that they are part of a spiritual family who share the same struggles and the same hope. When one suffers, the others lift him in prayer. When one stands firm, others are inspired to do the same. This is the spiritual solidarity of the Body of Christ.

Faithfulness also means refusing to compromise biblical convictions. The believer must not yield to the temptation of conformity or moral neutrality. Daniel, exiled in Babylon, refused to defile himself with the king's food (Daniel 1:8). His loyalty to Jehovah brought divine favor and protection. Likewise, Christians today must reject the world's moral corruption, choosing righteousness even when it costs reputation or comfort.

Joy Amid Hatred and Persecution

The paradox of Christian courage is that joy can coexist with suffering. Jesus told His followers, "Blessed are you when people insult you and persecute you and falsely say all kinds of evil against you because of me. Rejoice and be glad, for your reward is great in heaven" (Matthew 5:11–12). The believer's joy is not derived from circumstances but from his relationship with Christ and the hope of eternal life.

Paul and Silas, beaten and imprisoned in Philippi, sang hymns to God at midnight (Acts 16:25). Their joy was the fruit of faith, rooted in confidence that Jehovah was in control even amid injustice. The Holy Spirit produces this joy within those who obey the truth (Galatians 5:22). It is a supernatural gladness that defies worldly logic.

Persecution purifies faith. It removes superficial allegiance and reveals the authenticity of one's devotion to God. When the world's hatred intensifies, the believer's dependence upon Jehovah deepens. The joy that arises from this dependence transcends fear. It is the assurance that Christ has overcome the world and that no opposition can separate the believer from His love (Romans 8:35–39).

Furthermore, joy amid persecution is a testimony to the power of the Gospel. When unbelievers witness Christians enduring suffering with peace and grace, they see evidence that faith in Christ is real. The world may dismiss theological arguments, but it cannot ignore a life transformed by divine courage. Thus, joy in suffering becomes a form of evangelism, pointing others to the One who gives strength and peace beyond human comprehension.

Victory Over the World Through Faith

The Christian's courage ultimately rests upon the certainty of victory. The Apostle John declared, "For whatever is born of God overcomes the world; and this is the victory that has overcome the world—our faith" (1 John 5:4). Faith unites the believer with Christ, the Conqueror of sin, death, and Satan. Through His death and resurrection, Jesus triumphed over the world's rebellion, disarming the spiritual powers that opposed Jehovah's purpose (Colossians 2:15).

Victory over the world is not achieved through political power, human strategy, or cultural influence but through steadfast obedience to the Word of God. The believer conquers by remaining faithful to Christ in the face of opposition. Each act of obedience, each refusal to compromise, each proclamation of truth is a declaration of victory over the lies of the enemy.

Faith enables the believer to see beyond the visible and to rest in the unseen promises of God. The world may appear dominant, its systems powerful, its ideologies persuasive, but all of it is passing away (1 John 2:17). The Christian lives for an enduring kingdom—a kingdom that cannot be shaken. His courage is not blind optimism but confidence in the faithfulness of Jehovah, who will soon vindicate His people and bring everlasting peace through His Son.

When Christ returns to establish His Millennial Reign, those who have remained steadfast will share in His glory. They will no longer face hatred or persecution but will rejoice in the victory that faith has secured. Therefore, the believer today must hold fast, for the struggle is temporary but the triumph eternal.

Faith in Christ does not remove conflict with the world; it transforms it. It gives the believer strength to endure, wisdom to discern, and joy to persevere. In this present age of hostility, the call remains the same as it did in the first century: "Be strong and courageous. Do not be afraid or dismayed, for Jehovah your God is with you wherever you go" (Joshua 1:9).

To stand with Christ is to stand against the world, but it is also to stand in victory. The world's hatred is fleeting; God's approval is eternal. True courage, therefore, is not found in the absence of opposition but in unwavering faith that triumphs over it.

Chapter 7 – The Courage of Prayerful Dependence

Main Verse: "Do not be anxious about anything, but in everything by prayer and supplication with thanksgiving let your requests be made known to God." — *Philippians 4:6*

Prayer as a Source of Strength

The Christian's life is one of constant dependence upon Jehovah. True strength does not arise from self-sufficiency or human willpower but from humble communion with the Almighty through prayer. The Apostle Paul's exhortation to the Philippians embodies this truth: the believer is commanded not to be anxious but to bring all matters before God with thanksgiving. Prayer, therefore, is not an act of desperation, but a declaration of faith. It is the soul's reliance upon divine wisdom and power, demonstrating confidence that Jehovah governs all circumstances.

In prayer, the Christian acknowledges his weakness and Jehovah's strength. It is the spiritual exchange whereby the believer surrenders self-reliance and embraces divine sufficiency. Jesus Himself, though perfect, regularly withdrew to solitary places to pray (Luke 5:16), not out of necessity for repentance, but as a demonstration of continual dependence on His Father. His example reveals that prayer is not optional—it is essential. The believer's courage is born not from inward resolve, but from the assurance that Jehovah listens and acts according to His will. Prayer is the means by which the anxious heart becomes the steadfast heart, grounded in the knowledge that God's sovereignty exceeds human fear.

Fear Removed Through Fellowship with God

Fear thrives in isolation. When one turns inward and magnifies the uncertainties of life, the result is anxiety, confusion, and despair. But fellowship with Jehovah through prayer removes fear by restoring proper perspective. The Psalmist declared, "When I am afraid, I put my trust in You" (Psalm 56:3). This act of trust is cultivated through the intimacy of prayer, for prayer places the believer in direct communion with the Source of peace.

Through prayer, one learns to interpret life not through the lens of trouble, but through the promises of God. The believer who prays with understanding does not deny difficulty but views it under the authority of Jehovah's hand. As fear is displaced by faith, the heart finds calmness even in the storm. Fellowship with God does not eliminate suffering but transforms the believer's response to it. The Christian who prays faithfully walks in the awareness that Jehovah's presence is near, His care is constant, and His purposes are righteous.

Confidence in God's Answer

Confidence in prayer arises from a right understanding of Jehovah's character. The believer who knows God as both sovereign and loving prays not with uncertainty, but with reverent assurance. Jesus taught that "your Father knows what you need before you ask Him" (Matthew 6:8). This truth should never discourage prayer but should deepen it. Prayer is not to inform God of what He already knows, but to express dependence upon His will and delight in His fellowship.

Confidence does not mean expecting that God will always answer as one wishes, but rather that He will always answer rightly. The faithful Christian prays with submission to Jehovah's wisdom, knowing that divine love governs every delay, redirection, or denial. As the believer matures in faith, confidence in prayer grows—not because the believer's requests become perfect, but because his heart aligns increasingly with God's purposes. Such confidence dispels doubt and grants courage, for the one who prays in faith knows that Jehovah's response, in whatever form, is best.

This confidence is beautifully displayed in the life of Christ at Gethsemane. As He faced betrayal and death, He prayed, "Not as I will, but as You will" (Matthew 26:39). His prayer revealed both His anguish and His absolute trust. True confidence in prayer imitates this pattern—open, earnest, yet wholly submissive.

The Peace That Guards the Heart

Paul continues in Philippians 4:7, "And the peace of God, which surpasses all understanding, will guard your hearts and your minds in Christ Jesus." This peace is not the absence of conflict or trouble but the divine stability that stands guard over the believer's inner life. It is a supernatural calm, independent of external circumstances, grounded in faith that Jehovah reigns and that Christ intercedes.

This peace "guards" the heart as a sentinel—actively protecting the believer's thoughts from the invasion of fear and doubt. The Greek term used, *phroureō*, conveys the idea of a military garrison, showing that God's peace stands as an unshakable defense against the assaults of anxiety. When prayer is genuine and accompanied by thanksgiving, Jehovah responds not only with provision but with inward protection. The believer's courage is preserved by divine peace, and his joy remains steadfast even when his world is unsettled.

Such peace cannot be produced through philosophy, human reasoning, or positive thinking. It is the direct result of resting in Jehovah's promises. Isaiah declared, "You keep him in perfect peace whose mind is stayed on You, because he trusts in You" (Isaiah 26:3). The heart that remains fixed upon God through prayer experiences serenity that defies explanation, for it is guarded by the very peace of God Himself.

Persevering Prayer in Turbulent Times

Prayerful dependence must not be sporadic or seasonal; it must be consistent. Turbulent times often tempt believers to abandon prayer, supposing that silence or delay means divine absence. Yet Scripture reveals that the opposite is true—Jehovah honors persistent prayer. Jesus illustrated this in the parable of the persistent widow (Luke 18:1–8), teaching "that they ought always to pray and not lose heart." Perseverance in prayer demonstrates faith's endurance.

When the believer faces affliction, persecution, or uncertainty, he must press onward in prayer. The habit of continual prayer keeps the heart aligned with God's purposes and prevents discouragement from taking root. The courage of prayerful dependence is not displayed by instant deliverance but by steadfastness in seeking Jehovah's will. Through enduring prayer, the believer learns to rely on God's strength rather than his own resolve.

Turbulent times reveal the reality of one's faith. Those who persevere in prayer testify that their confidence is not shaken by temporary trials. Prayer in such moments becomes both refuge and reinforcement—it shelters the soul and fortifies courage. The believer who continues in prayer, even when answers seem distant, will find that God's presence sustains him through every storm.

Trusting Jehovah's Timing and Will

One of the greatest tests of faith is waiting upon Jehovah's timing. The natural heart desires immediate answers, but divine wisdom operates according to perfect timing and purpose. To trust Jehovah's timing is to recognize that His understanding transcends human comprehension. Ecclesiastes 3:11 affirms, "He has made everything beautiful in its time." This truth assures the believer that delay is not neglect, but purposeful refinement.

Trusting God's timing in prayer cultivates patience and humility. The believer learns that prayer is not a mechanism for controlling outcomes but a means of conforming the will to Jehovah's. As Jesus trusted His Father's timing in every aspect of His ministry, so the Christian must rest in the assurance that God acts neither too soon nor too late. The unseen purposes of Jehovah's delays often prepare the believer for blessings he could not yet bear or for growth he has not yet achieved.

Submission to Jehovah's will is the highest expression of faith. When prayer ends with "Your will be done," it is not resignation but triumph—the yielding of the human heart to divine perfection. The believer who trusts God's will finds rest even before the answer comes, for he knows that whatever God ordains is right. True courage, therefore, is not found in striving for control, but in resting in confident surrender to the sovereign will of Jehovah.

Chapter 8 – Standing Firm Against Satan's Attacks

Main Verse: "Resist the devil, and he will flee from you." — James 4:7

Recognizing the Enemy's Schemes

The apostle James provides the Christian with one of the most vital imperatives in spiritual warfare: "Resist the devil." This command reveals that believers are not helpless in the face of Satan's efforts to undermine their faith. Rather, the believer, strengthened by Jehovah through His Word, is called to recognize, expose, and stand firm against the devil's schemes. Satan, whose very name means "Adversary," is the chief opposer of Jehovah's purposes and of those who seek to serve Him. He is not a mere symbolic representation of evil, but a real, intelligent, and malicious spiritual being who has rebelled against God. Jesus called him "the father of the lie" (John 8:44), indicating his principal weapon: deception.

From the very beginning, Satan's strategy has been to cast doubt upon Jehovah's Word, as seen in the Garden of Eden when he said to Eve, "Did God actually say...?" (Genesis 3:1). This questioning of divine truth remains his foremost tactic. He seeks to infiltrate the mind and corrupt the heart by suggesting that obedience to God is restrictive, unnecessary, or outdated. Thus, every follower of Christ must train the mind to recognize falsehood and resist compromise. The apostle Paul warned that "we are not ignorant of his designs" (2 Corinthians 2:11). These designs include deceit through false doctrines, temptation through moral corruption, and distraction through worldly cares.

Satan's attacks are often subtle, appealing to human desires, pride, or emotional vulnerability. He disguises himself as "an angel of light" (2 Corinthians 11:14), presenting error as truth and rebellion as liberation. His methods are calculated to distort God's standards, so that sin becomes normalized and righteousness appears extreme. Recognizing his schemes demands discernment grounded in Scripture. Only by consistent study, meditation, and obedience to the Word can believers expose Satan's disguises.

The Battle of the Mind and Heart

The true battlefield of spiritual warfare is not physical but mental and moral. The mind is where truth is either accepted or rejected, and the heart is where loyalty is tested. Paul wrote, "For though we walk in the flesh, we are not waging war according to the flesh... we destroy arguments and every lofty opinion raised against the knowledge of God, and take every thought captive to obey Christ" (2 Corinthians 10:3–5). The devil's chief aim is to infiltrate the believer's thought life with doubt, fear, lust, resentment, or pride, thereby weakening devotion to Jehovah.

Satan knows that if he can corrupt the believer's mind, he can influence conduct. For this reason, guarding the heart and mind through prayer and Scriptural meditation is essential. Philippians 4:6–7 teaches, "Do not be anxious about anything, but in everything by prayer and supplication with thanksgiving let your requests be made known to God. And the peace of God, which surpasses all understanding, will guard your hearts and your minds in Christ Jesus." That "peace of God" functions as a spiritual fortress that shields believers from the assaults of discouragement and doubt.

The heart, in Scripture, represents the seat of affection, will, and moral direction. When the heart becomes divided between devotion to God and attachment to the world, Satan gains a foothold. Jesus warned, "No one can serve two masters" (Matthew 6:24). Thus, the believer must keep a single-minded focus on Jehovah's will, rejecting the enticements of materialism, immorality, and self-centered ambition. When the mind and heart remain aligned with divine truth, Satan's attacks lose their power.

The Armor of God as Protection

Paul's description of the "armor of God" in Ephesians 6:10–18 provides a complete defense against the devil's attacks. "Put on the whole armor of God, that you may be able to stand against the schemes of the devil," he writes. Each element of the armor corresponds to a vital aspect of Christian steadfastness.

The "belt of truth" holds everything together, for only by commitment to divine truth can believers stand firm. The "breastplate of righteousness" protects the heart from moral compromise, preserving integrity before Jehovah. The "shoes of readiness given by the gospel of peace" enable believers to stand firm and move forward in their mission of proclaiming the good news, unshaken by persecution or opposition. The "shield of faith" extinguishes all the flaming arrows of the evil one—those sudden attacks of fear, doubt, or temptation. The "helmet of salvation" guards the mind with assurance of Jehovah's promises, and the "sword of the Spirit," which is the Word of God, is both defensive and offensive, enabling believers to cut through deception and proclaim truth.

The armor must be worn daily. Spiritual negligence invites vulnerability. Satan attacks the unguarded mind through compromise, distraction, or sin left unconfessed. Constant prayer, study, and obedience are the means of keeping the armor intact. The apostle urges, "Pray at all times in the Spirit, with all prayer and supplication." This does not refer to mystical experience, but to praying in harmony with the guidance of the Spirit-inspired Word.

Faith as a Shield Against Fear

Faith, described by Paul as a shield, plays a unique role in neutralizing Satan's fiery assaults. It is through faith that the believer trusts Jehovah's promises even when circumstances appear dire. Fear is one of Satan's most effective tools, for fear weakens resolve, clouds judgment, and leads to spiritual paralysis. When Peter began to sink upon the sea, it was not because the waves grew stronger but because his faith wavered (Matthew 14:30–31). In contrast, strong faith is unwavering confidence in Jehovah's power, wisdom, and goodness, even when the outcome is unseen.

Hebrews 11 provides numerous examples of faith in action—men and women who, though imperfect, trusted Jehovah despite immense opposition. Faith not only protects against external threats but also quenches internal anxieties. Isaiah 26:3 assures, "You keep him in perfect peace whose mind is stayed on You, because he trusts in You." The shield of faith is strengthened through regular engagement with God's Word, for "faith comes from hearing, and hearing through the word of Christ" (Romans 10:17).

Satan's objective is to erode that faith by promoting skepticism, discouragement, or disappointment. He whispers, "God has forgotten you," or "Your prayers are futile." The believer must counter these lies with Scripture, just as Jesus did during His temptation in the wilderness (Matthew 4:1–11). Each response of Christ began with, "It is written," showing that the Word of God is the surest defense against doubt. Faith is not blind optimism; it is intelligent reliance on the unchangeable character of Jehovah and His revealed Word.

Maintaining Purity Under Assault

One of Satan's most persistent strategies is moral corruption. He seeks to defile what is pure, to trivialize holiness, and to enslave the mind to sinful desires. In a world saturated with sensuality, deceit, and irreverence, maintaining moral purity requires vigilance and determination. The apostle Peter warns, "Be sober-minded; be watchful. Your adversary the devil prowls around like a roaring lion, seeking someone to devour" (1 Peter 5:8). Satan's roar is often disguised in entertainment, social trends, or cultural pressures that normalize sin.

Purity is not merely abstaining from outward sin; it involves maintaining inner cleanliness of thought and motive. Jesus said, "Blessed are the pure in heart, for they shall see God" (Matthew 5:8). Purity is cultivated through continual cleansing by the Word of God. Psalm 119:9 declares, "How can a young man keep his way pure? By guarding it according to your word." The believer must be disciplined in rejecting any influence that dulls the conscience or fosters impurity. This includes choosing associations, media, and habits that honor Jehovah rather than gratify the flesh.

Sexual immorality, pride, greed, and dishonesty are among Satan's favorite tools. He exploits natural desires by twisting them into disobedience. Yet the Holy Scriptures provide both warning and hope: "No temptation has overtaken you that is not common to man. God is faithful, and He will not let you be tempted beyond your ability, but with the temptation He will also provide the way of escape"

(1 Corinthians 10:13). The way of escape is found through prayer, Scripture, and fellowship with faithful believers who encourage righteousness.

Courage Through Spiritual Vigilance

Standing firm against Satan requires courage grounded in spiritual vigilance. The Christian life is not a passive existence but an active stand against evil. Paul exhorted the Corinthians, "Be watchful, stand firm in the faith, act like men, be strong" (1 Corinthians 16:13). Such vigilance involves continual awareness that the world lies under Satan's influence (1 John 5:19). Yet believers are not to fear, for Jehovah has provided every resource needed to remain faithful.

Courage arises not from self-confidence but from confidence in Jehovah's sovereign power. When David faced Goliath, his courage was not in his own ability but in his conviction that "the battle is Jehovah's" (1 Samuel 17:47). In the same way, every believer faces spiritual giants in the form of temptation, persecution, or discouragement, yet victory is assured to those who rely on God's strength.

Prayerful alertness is essential. Jesus told His disciples, "Watch and pray that you may not enter into temptation" (Matthew 26:41). This watchfulness is not fear-driven but faith-driven, keeping the believer sensitive to danger and responsive to God's direction. When courage is anchored in truth, righteousness, faith, and salvation, Satan's assaults cannot prevail.

The believer must therefore cultivate an unbroken relationship with Jehovah through constant prayer and obedience. The more one walks in harmony with God's Word, the less room Satan finds to operate. James' counsel summarizes this perfectly: "Submit yourselves therefore to God. Resist the devil, and he will flee from you" (James 4:7). Submission to Jehovah precedes resistance; when the heart is fully yielded to His will, Satan cannot withstand the authority of divine truth.

To stand firm against Satan's attacks is to live daily in the strength of Jehovah's provision, clothed in His armor, guided by His Word, and sustained by faith. Victory is not uncertain—it is promised to all who remain steadfast, obedient, and alert. The devil will flee, not because of human strength, but because he cannot endure the presence of unwavering faith in the Almighty.

Chapter 9 – Courage to Confess Christ Publicly

Main Verse: "Whoever confesses me before men, I will also confess before my Father who is in heaven." — Matthew 10:32

In a world where following Christ can make you stand out, being bold in your faith takes real courage. Jesus' words in Matthew 10:32 are not just a statement of encouragement—they are a call to action. Confessing Christ before others means declaring your loyalty to Him openly and without shame, even when it costs something. For young believers, this is one of the most powerful ways to show true discipleship.

Boldness in Witnessing

Being bold for Christ does not mean being loud or argumentative; it means being confident in the truth you believe. The apostles were examples of this kind of courage. After the resurrection, Peter and John faced threats from the religious leaders who demanded that they stop speaking about Jesus. But they answered, "We cannot stop speaking about what we have seen and heard" (Acts 4:20). Their confidence came not from pride but from conviction. They had witnessed the risen Christ, and that truth burned so deeply in their hearts that silence was not an option.

For young Christians today, boldness means standing up for what is right when others laugh or stay silent. It means speaking truth about Jesus when people distort or mock His message. True boldness is not natural; it comes from knowing Jehovah and trusting His power more than fearing the opinions of others.

When a student defends biblical truth in class, or a teen speaks about their faith online without compromise, that is real courage. It shows that Christ means more to them than popularity, comfort, or acceptance. Jesus never said that confessing Him would be easy, but He promised that it would be rewarded.

Overcoming the Fear of Man

Fear of what people think can be one of the greatest obstacles to confessing Christ. Proverbs 29:25 warns, "The fear of man brings a snare, but whoever trusts in Jehovah will be safe." Fear of rejection, ridicule, or exclusion often silences believers, especially young ones who desire to be liked. Yet, every follower of Christ must choose whom to fear more—people or God.

When Daniel was threatened with death for praying to Jehovah, he continued his worship openly, knowing the cost. His courage did not come from being fearless but from trusting God more than men. Similarly, Jesus said, "Do not be afraid of those who kill the body but cannot kill the soul; rather, fear Him who can destroy both soul and body in Gehenna" (Matthew 10:28).

Fear loses its power when faith grows stronger. The more you know Christ through Scripture, the less the world's opinions control you. Prayer and meditation on God's Word build spiritual confidence. When the Word fills your heart, fear of man fades because you realize that eternity matters more than temporary approval.

Confession as a Test of Genuine Faith

Confession is more than words; it reveals what truly lives in the heart. Romans 10:9 says, "If you confess with your mouth that Jesus is Lord and believe in your heart that God raised Him from the dead, you will be saved." Confession flows naturally from genuine belief. If someone truly loves Christ, that love will eventually be spoken aloud.

Those who claim to follow Christ but remain silent in public about their faith are often guided by fear or compromise. But Jesus said clearly, "Whoever denies me before men, I will also deny before my Father who is in heaven" (Matthew 10:33). To deny Christ is not only to say "I don't believe," but also to refuse to stand with Him when faith is tested.

Young Christians should remember that silence can sometimes speak loudly. Refusing to acknowledge Christ when given the opportunity can be a quiet form of denial. True faith confesses Christ with conviction because it understands that salvation and allegiance are inseparable.

Confession is also a sign of belonging. By publicly identifying with Christ, you declare that your loyalty belongs to Him, not to this world. That kind of open confession shows that your faith is real and alive.

Speaking Truth in a Culture of Silence

The culture today pressures everyone—especially youth—to conform. The message is simple: keep your faith private, keep your opinions soft, and never speak against what the world celebrates. But Jesus never called His followers to be silent. He said, "You are the light of the world. A city set on a hill cannot be hidden" (Matthew 5:14).

Being light means shining truth even when the world prefers darkness. This includes speaking up for biblical truth about morality, creation, and salvation, even if it means standing alone. Truth spoken with humility and love still offends those who resist God, but it must be spoken nonetheless.

Paul encouraged Timothy, a young man in ministry, to be courageous: "Do not be ashamed of the testimony about our Lord" (2 Timothy 1:8). Shame silences believers, but courage sets them apart. The culture of silence will always exist, but the voice of truth must be louder—not in arrogance, but in conviction.

When you speak God's truth, do so with gentleness and respect (1 Peter 3:15). The goal is not to win arguments but to glorify Christ and reach others with His message.

The Cost and Reward of Open Faith

There is a cost to following Christ publicly. Jesus said, "If anyone wants to come after me, let him deny himself, take up his cross, and follow me" (Matthew 16:24). For young people, this cost might come through social rejection, mockery, or exclusion. In some parts of the world, it may even lead to persecution. Yet the reward far outweighs the cost.

Jesus promised that those who confess Him before others will be confessed before the Father. Imagine that moment: the Son of God standing before the throne of Jehovah, declaring your name because you were not ashamed of His. That eternal reward cannot compare to any temporary discomfort here on earth.

Open faith also strengthens others. When one person stands up for Christ, it gives courage to others who are watching. Your example might inspire a friend to start reading the Bible, attend worship, or stand up for truth themselves. Public confession multiplies faith because courage is contagious.

Every generation of believers has had to decide whether to live boldly for Christ or quietly blend into the crowd. Today's youth face new challenges—social media pressure, moral confusion, and widespread unbelief—but the same choice remains: will you confess Christ openly?

Living as a Testimony of Courage

Your daily life can be a confession of Christ even without words. The way you speak, dress, act, and treat others reveals whether you belong to Him. Jesus said, "Let your light shine before men, so that they may see your good works and give glory to your Father who is in heaven" (Matthew 5:16). When you live with integrity, kindness, and purity, people notice the difference—and that opens doors to speak about your faith.

Living courageously for Christ means not compromising your convictions for acceptance. It means resisting temptation, refusing immoral trends, and choosing to live by God's standards. Such living declares, "Christ rules my life."

This kind of testimony is powerful because it reflects the reality of transformation. When others see peace, joy, and purpose in your life, they see the evidence of faith that cannot be hidden. The courage to confess Christ publicly begins with a heart fully devoted to Him, guided by His Word, and strengthened through prayer.

FEARLESS

Jehovah honors those who stand firm. No act of confession is ever forgotten by Him. Even a single word of faith spoken in a moment of pressure is precious in His sight. Young believer, you may feel alone when you stand for Christ, but you are never truly alone. The same Lord who gave courage to Daniel, Peter, and Timothy stands with you today. Be bold. Speak truth. Live unashamed. Confess Christ before men—and He will confess you before His Father in heaven.

Chapter 10 – Courage Through Purity and Integrity

Main Verse: "The righteous are as bold as a lion." — *Proverbs 28:1*

The Moral Courage to Stand for Truth

Moral courage does not emerge from self-confidence or the praise of others but from the conviction that one stands in harmony with the truth of God's Word. The proverb states that "the righteous are as bold as a lion," showing that true boldness arises not from arrogance but from righteousness—right standing with Jehovah through faith and obedience. The righteous man's courage is not reckless; it is rooted in a conscience aligned with divine standards. Throughout Scripture, the people of God demonstrated courage when they upheld truth against corruption, idolatry, and moral compromise. Daniel, for instance, exhibited moral courage when he refused to defile himself with the king's delicacies (Daniel 1:8). His courage was not in defiance of authority for its own sake but in obedience to Jehovah's commands regarding purity.

Moral courage is the willingness to act in accordance with God's truth even when such action brings ridicule, rejection, or persecution. The apostles in the first century modeled this when they declared before the Sanhedrin, "We must obey God as ruler rather than men" (Acts 5:29). Their integrity was tested, but their faithfulness revealed the kind of courage that cannot be subdued by fear. In every generation, the righteous face pressure to conform to falsehood, immorality, and worldly compromise. Yet, like the lion who does not retreat in the face of danger, those who walk in truth cannot be silenced when the honor of Jehovah is at stake.

Courage built upon purity and integrity means that the believer fears sin more than suffering, dishonor more than death, and disobedience more than persecution. The world equates courage with physical strength or emotional boldness, but the Bible teaches that true bravery arises from moral purity. The one who walks uprightly before God possesses a strength that no external power can erode. When the conscience is undefiled, the heart stands firm in the day of testing.

Edward D. Andrews

Integrity in Private and Public Life

Integrity is the backbone of Christian character. It signifies a consistent, undivided heart devoted to righteousness whether seen or unseen. Many display outward piety but lack inward faithfulness. The person of integrity lives the same before men as before God, understanding that Jehovah searches the heart (Jeremiah 17:10). When the psalmist prayed, "Examine me, O Jehovah, and put me to the test; refine my kidneys and my heart" (Psalm 26:2), he expressed the essence of true integrity—willingness to be transparent before God.

Integrity in private life ensures that hidden sins do not erode spiritual confidence. A double life always weakens courage. When David sinned secretly, he confessed that his vitality was drained and his bones wasted away through groaning (Psalm 32:3). Guilt produces timidity; unconfessed sin robs the believer of spiritual boldness. But when integrity governs both thought and action, peace of mind and spiritual strength are preserved.

Public integrity manifests itself in the believer's dealings with others—in honesty, fairness, and reliability. The righteous man's word is dependable because he fears Jehovah. The apostle Paul instructed, "Provide fine works in the sight of all men" (Romans 12:17). Integrity, then, is not only inward but also visible in daily conduct. Christians must resist the moral fragmentation of modern society, where deceit and compromise are considered acceptable tools for advancement. Jehovah demands complete integrity: "He who walks blamelessly will remain in safety, but he whose ways are crooked will suddenly fall" (Proverbs 28:18).

Integrity joins with courage, for it takes spiritual bravery to maintain honesty in a world that rewards deceit. Yet integrity cannot exist without purity of heart. The believer who lives in holiness finds his courage renewed, for he knows he has nothing to conceal and nothing to fear.

The Fearless Conscience of the Righteous

The conscience, when informed by Scripture, becomes a powerful ally in cultivating fearless faith. The conscience of the righteous is fearless because it rests upon the certainty of divine approval. Such a conscience is not self-made but trained through God's Word. The apostle Paul declared, "Our boast is this, the testimony of our conscience, that in simplicity and godly sincerity, not by fleshly wisdom but by the grace of God, we have conducted ourselves in the world" (2 Corinthians 1:12).

When the conscience is clear before Jehovah, there is a serenity that no accusation can disturb. Fear and guilt are the fruit of a compromised conscience, but boldness and peace come from one made pure through repentance and faith. A righteous conscience fears only displeasing God. This fear produces not cowardice but wisdom, for it guards against sin and cultivates moral stability.

The fearless conscience stands unmoved in times of accusation or hostility. When Daniel faced the lions' den, he did so without trembling because his conscience was unblemished before Jehovah and men (Daniel 6:22). The strength of his conviction made him unafraid of death. The righteous today need the same fearless conscience—a mind governed by truth and a heart purified by obedience. In an era where sin is rationalized and truth is relativized, the believer's only security lies in a conscience that answers first to God.

Purity in a Corrupt Generation

The moral decay of modern society parallels the conditions of ancient times when "every inclination of the thoughts of [man's] heart was only bad all the time" (Genesis 6:5). Yet Jehovah calls His people to live as "blameless and innocent, children of God without blemish in the midst of a crooked and twisted generation" (Philippians 2:15). Purity of heart, speech, and action is not optional for those who belong to Christ—it is essential. The believer cannot radiate light while mingling with the darkness of moral compromise.

Purity begins in the heart. Jesus taught, "Blessed are the pure in heart, for they will see God" (Matthew 5:8). The heart purified by faith rejects sinful desire and guards against impurity in thought and behavior. In a world saturated with immorality and corruption, purity demands vigilance. The Christian must guard his eyes, speech, and associations, avoiding what defiles both mind and conscience.

Purity also strengthens moral courage. The one whose heart is clean before God can face hostility without fear, for his motives are undefiled. Joseph, when tempted by Potiphar's wife, resisted not because of social consequences but because he would not sin against God (Genesis 39:9). His purity gave him the courage to flee rather than compromise. The believer who seeks purity through the Word of God and prayer gains inner fortitude that sustains him amid temptation.

The corrupt generation in which we live glorifies self-gratification, mocks chastity, and scorns moral boundaries. Yet purity is the true path to freedom. The impure are slaves to passion and deception, but those who pursue holiness enjoy peace and power from Jehovah. To live pure in an impure age is an act of courage, one that honors the Creator and bears witness to His transforming grace.

Faithfulness in All Circumstances

Faithfulness is the enduring expression of courage and integrity. It is steadfast loyalty to God regardless of changing conditions or personal cost. In Scripture, faithfulness is portrayed as a lifelong commitment rather than a fleeting emotion. Daniel, Joseph, Ruth, and the apostles exemplified unwavering faithfulness under pressure. They demonstrated that faithfulness is not measured by ease but by endurance.

The righteous remain faithful because they trust in Jehovah's justice and sovereignty. They do not interpret trials as abandonment but as opportunities to glorify God through steadfastness. The apostle Paul, even while imprisoned, rejoiced that the gospel continued to advance (Philippians 1:12-14). His courage stemmed from faithfulness that no chain could restrain.

Faithfulness in all circumstances also includes consistency in small duties. Jesus taught, "He who is faithful in what is least is faithful also in much" (Luke 16:10). Courage is not only required in public battles but also in private obedience. The believer who remains faithful in the hidden disciplines of prayer, honesty, and purity will be bold when greater tests come.

The strength of faithfulness lies in dependence upon Jehovah. The Christian does not rely on personal resolve alone but on divine help. Jehovah provides the endurance necessary to remain steadfast when others yield to fear or compromise. Faithfulness, then, becomes a reflection of God's own unchanging character in the life of the believer.

The Strength That Comes from a Clean Heart

Spiritual strength flows from moral cleanliness. David prayed, "Create in me a clean heart, O God, and put within me a new spirit" (Psalm 51:10). A clean heart renews courage because it restores fellowship with Jehovah. Sin divides the heart, corrupts the motives, and weakens resolve. Repentance restores integrity and enables the believer to act with spiritual confidence.

The clean heart is fearless because it trusts completely in Jehovah's approval rather than human opinion. Isaiah wrote, "You will keep in perfect peace the one whose mind is steadfast, because he trusts in you" (Isaiah 26:3). Peace of mind and boldness of spirit belong to those whose hearts are clean through obedience. The strength of the righteous does not come from worldly status or physical might but from a conscience at rest in God's favor.

Purity, integrity, and courage are inseparable. Each strengthens the other, forming a life of spiritual resilience. The pure heart produces integrity; integrity fuels courage; courage sustains faithfulness. Together, they make the believer "as bold as a lion." Such boldness is not loud or boastful but calm, resolute, and enduring—the quiet strength of one who knows Jehovah and walks uprightly before Him.

The clean heart does not tremble before adversity, for it is anchored in the righteousness of Christ. As the apostle Paul affirmed, "I can do all things through him who gives me strength" (Philippians 4:13). That strength flows from a life purified by obedience, upheld by faith, and governed by love for Jehovah. The world may mock purity and despise integrity, but the believer who walks in righteousness possesses a courage that no fear can overthrow and no corruption can taint.

Edward D. Andrews

Chapter 11 – Courage in the Face of Death

Main Verse: "For to me to live is Christ, and to die is gain." — Philippians 1:21

The Christian View of Death

The apostle Paul's declaration in Philippians 1:21 captures the essence of Christian courage in the face of death. For the believer, life is an opportunity to glorify Christ, and death is not loss but gain. This is a radical redefinition of human mortality, one that can only be embraced through the lens of divine revelation. Death entered the world through Adam's sin, and as Romans 5:12 declares, "through one man sin entered into the world, and death through sin, and so death spread to all men because all sinned." Death is therefore not a natural transition but the enemy of human life, a curse resulting from rebellion against Jehovah. Yet for those reconciled to God through Christ, death loses its terror.

The world views death as the ultimate end, the extinguishing of self. Many philosophies and religions have sought to romanticize or redefine death, but Scripture maintains its clarity—death is separation from life, not transformation into another form of existence. Ecclesiastes 9:5 affirms that "the dead know nothing," emphasizing that human consciousness ceases in death. The Christian hope does not rest in an immortal soul escaping the body but in the resurrection that Jehovah promises. Thus, when Paul says "to die is gain," he speaks not of immediate heavenly existence but of the assurance that death cannot separate him from the love of God in Christ Jesus (Romans 8:38–39).

This confidence rests upon the truth that life belongs to God. The believer's existence is bound to Christ. "For you died, and your life has been hidden with Christ in God" (Colossians 3:3). Therefore, death is not a loss of life's purpose but a seal upon a life lived in faithful service to the Master. To live is Christ because every breath is devoted to His will; to die is gain because it brings rest from labor and a certain expectation of resurrection.

Deliverance from the Fear of the Grave

Humanity's greatest fear has always been death. The grave—Sheol or Hades in Scripture—was viewed as the shadowy realm where all humans descend. Before Christ's resurrection, even righteous men like Job, David, and Hezekiah expressed anguish at the thought of dying. Job cried out, "If a man dies, will he live again?" (Job 14:14). Yet Job's question was prophetic, pointing toward the resurrection hope later fulfilled in Christ.

Hebrews 2:14–15 reveals how Christ's victory liberated believers from this bondage: "Since therefore the children share in flesh and blood, He Himself likewise partook of the same things, that through death He might destroy the one having the power of death, that is, the devil, and deliver all those who through fear of death were subject to lifelong slavery." Satan used death as a weapon, keeping mankind enslaved through the dread of the unknown. But Christ entered death voluntarily, broke its power, and rose to everlasting life. By conquering death, He removed its sting.

This deliverance is not an emotional denial of mortality but a reasoned assurance grounded in Scripture. The believer knows that the grave cannot hold those whom Jehovah will raise. Just as Christ's tomb was empty on the third day, so all who belong to Him will one day hear His voice and come forth (John 5:28–29). The fear of death is replaced with confident faith, for "death has been swallowed up in victory" (1 Corinthians 15:54).

For the Christian, courage in facing death comes from understanding that it cannot interrupt the divine plan. Death is a defeated foe, an enemy soon to be abolished completely (1 Corinthians 15:26). Thus, believers do not live in terror of their mortality but in expectation of the resurrection to everlasting life.

Resurrection as the Foundation of Hope

The resurrection of Jesus Christ is the cornerstone of Christian courage in the face of death. Without it, faith would be futile. As Paul states clearly, "If Christ has not been raised, your faith is worthless; you are still in your sins" (1 Corinthians 15:17). The resurrection is not merely a comforting doctrine but the divine guarantee that death does not have the final word.

Jesus' resurrection was not symbolic. It was bodily, historical, and verifiable. His empty tomb and post-resurrection appearances provide the foundation for Christian assurance. He Himself declared, "I am the resurrection and the life; whoever believes in Me, though he die, yet shall he live" (John 11:25). This statement was made before He raised Lazarus, proving His authority over death even before His own triumph at Calvary.

The believer's hope, therefore, is not vague immortality but the promise of being made alive again, restored to perfect life on a renewed earth. Paul describes this vividly in 1 Thessalonians 4:16–17: "For the Lord Himself will descend from heaven with a cry of command, with the voice of an archangel, and with the trumpet of God. And the dead in Christ will rise first." Resurrection means full restoration of life, not escape from the body but redemption of it.

This hope transforms the Christian's perspective on mortality. When the body ages or succumbs to illness, faith recalls the promise that "He who raised Christ Jesus from the dead will also give life to your mortal bodies through His Spirit who dwells in you" (Romans 8:11). Thus, death is seen not as annihilation but as a temporary sleep from which Jehovah will awaken His faithful servants.

Living Each Day with Eternity in View

Understanding the certainty of resurrection compels believers to live with eternity in view. Paul's attitude in Philippians 1:21 reflects a life wholly surrendered to Christ's purposes. He viewed earthly existence as a platform for service, not self-preservation. "If I am to live in the flesh, that means fruitful labor for me" (Philippians 1:22). Every day was an opportunity to magnify Christ, whether through preaching, suffering, or even dying for His name.

Such a perspective produces a life of fearless obedience. Those who live for eternity are not controlled by temporal fears. Jesus commanded His followers, "Do not fear those who kill the body but cannot kill the soul; rather fear Him who can destroy both soul and body in Gehenna" (Matthew

10:28). The righteous fear of Jehovah liberates the believer from the fear of man and death.

Living with eternity in view also nurtures spiritual vigilance. The Christian knows that his time is short and that Christ could return at any moment. This awareness motivates holiness, compassion, and steadfastness in ministry. As Paul admonished in 1 Corinthians 15:58, "Therefore, my beloved brothers, be steadfast, immovable, always abounding in the work of the Lord, knowing that your labor is not in vain in the Lord."

To live each day in light of eternity is to cultivate heavenly-mindedness while fulfilling earthly responsibilities. It means pursuing righteousness, evangelizing the lost, comforting the afflicted, and preparing for the day when Christ will call His own from the grave.

Courage in the Shadow of Mortality

True courage does not deny fear but overcomes it through faith. Every human being faces the reality of mortality. Even the strongest hearts tremble when confronted with death's inevitability. Yet the Christian's courage rests upon the unshakable conviction that Jehovah holds life and death in His hands. Psalm 31:15 declares, "My times are in Your hand." The believer does not need to know when or how death will come, for he knows the One who conquered it.

Paul faced execution under Nero's regime, yet he wrote to Timothy with calm assurance: "The time of my departure has come. I have fought the good fight, I have finished the race, I have kept the faith" (2 Timothy 4:6–7). His courage was not self-generated but rooted in faith in Jehovah's promises. Courage, therefore, is the fruit of trust.

When Stephen, the first Christian martyr, faced death by stoning, he fixed his eyes on Christ and said, "Lord Jesus, receive my spirit" (Acts 7:59). He faced death not with dread but with devotion. His final vision of Christ standing at the right hand of God confirmed his faith that death could not sever him from divine fellowship.

Believers today draw the same courage from the knowledge that Christ's resurrection guarantees their own. Though the body returns to dust, the promise of life remains secure. As the psalmist declared, "God will redeem my soul from the power of Sheol, for He will receive me" (Psalm 49:15). Courage in the shadow of mortality arises from confidence in divine redemption.

Victory Through Christ Over Death

The ultimate triumph belongs to Christ. His death was substitutionary—He bore the penalty of sin that brings death. His resurrection was victorious—He shattered the grip of the grave. Through Him, believers participate in this victory. "Thanks be to God, who gives us the victory through our Lord Jesus Christ" (1 Corinthians 15:57).

Christ's victory is not theoretical; it is experiential for all who belong to Him. Sin's power is broken, and death's dominion is undone. When the final resurrection occurs, Jehovah's plan for humanity will be complete, and death itself will be abolished forever. Revelation 21:4 promises, "He will wipe away every tear from their eyes, and death shall be no more."

This victory empowers the believer to face death not as a tyrant but as a conquered foe. Courage flows from knowing that nothing—not even death—can separate us from the love of God in Christ Jesus. Those who die in faith rest in Jehovah's memory, awaiting the call of life.

Therefore, the Christian can say with Paul, "For to me to live is Christ, and to die is gain." Life's purpose and death's promise both center upon the same Person—the risen Lord. To live is to serve Him faithfully; to die is to await the reward of everlasting life in His renewed creation. In both, Christ is magnified. This is the courage that defies the grave, born of faith in the One who lives forever.

Edward D. Andrews

Chapter 12 – Courage Through Fellowship and the Congregation

Main Verse: "And let us consider one another to stir up love and good works." — Hebrews 10:24

The Strength of Christian Unity

The inspired words of Hebrews 10:24 call upon Christians to look beyond themselves and to actively consider their brothers and sisters in the faith. The Christian life was never meant to be lived in isolation. The early congregation understood that fellowship was the spiritual oxygen that sustained courage in the face of opposition. When the writer of Hebrews exhorted believers to "consider one another," the command was not a mere suggestion of politeness or friendliness. It was a divine imperative that pointed to the vital necessity of community life.

True unity within the congregation does not arise from human effort or emotional affinity; it flows from the shared relationship with Christ Jesus as Head of the congregation. He prayed that His followers "may be one" (John 17:21), indicating that unity is both spiritual and practical. It is grounded in truth, for Jesus said, "Your word is truth" (John 17:17). Therefore, Christian unity is not a superficial agreement to coexist but a deep alignment in doctrine, purpose, and love. The strength of this unity fortifies believers against discouragement, fear, and compromise.

The Apostle Paul consistently emphasized this collective identity, likening the congregation to a body where every member has a distinct but necessary function (1 Corinthians 12:12–27). When believers dwell together in unity, as Psalm 133 declares, Jehovah's blessing rests upon them. Their fellowship becomes a channel of divine strength, enabling each member to endure hardship, proclaim truth, and persevere in righteousness. Courage is not born in solitude but grows where mutual love and faith reinforce one another.

Encouragement from Fellow Believers

Encouragement is a sacred ministry within the congregation. Hebrews 10:25 continues, "not forsaking our own assembling together, as is the habit of some, but encouraging one another." The writer understood that neglecting fellowship weakens spiritual resolve. The first-century Christians met frequently, despite persecution, because they drew courage and hope from one another. Their meetings were not social gatherings but moments of strengthening through prayer, Scripture reading, teaching, and mutual care.

Encouragement from fellow believers reflects the heart of Christ Himself, who continually strengthened His disciples. He reassured them when they faltered, corrected them when they erred, and prayed for them when they faced trials. In the same way, the congregation becomes an extension of His presence. Through words of faith, practical help, and shared burdens, Christians build each other up (1 Thessalonians 5:11).

True encouragement is not flattery but a deliberate act to fortify faith and character. When a believer feels the pressures of a godless world, another's steadfast faith becomes a testimony of Jehovah's sustaining power. This is why Proverbs 27:17 declares, "As iron sharpens iron, so one man sharpens another." The sharpening process involves friction, meaning that honest correction and exhortation also play a role in encouragement. A congregation marked by such spiritual interaction is not easily shaken; its members walk with courage because they walk together.

Standing Shoulder to Shoulder in Faith

In Philippians 1:27, Paul urges the believers to "stand firm in one spirit, with one mind striving together for the faith of the gospel." The imagery here evokes soldiers standing in formation, shoulder to shoulder, united under one cause. The spiritual battle demands such solidarity. Satan, the adversary, seeks to isolate individuals, knowing that separation from the body often leads to vulnerability. But when believers stand united, their courage is multiplied.

This collective strength is not achieved through mere human coordination but through the shared conviction that Christ reigns supreme and that His promises never fail. Courage is not the absence of fear but steadfastness despite it. When one believer falters, another steadies him; when one faces sorrow, another brings comfort. Together, they reflect the divine pattern of mutual support seen in the early church: "They devoted themselves to the apostles' teaching and to fellowship, to the breaking of bread and to prayer" (Acts 2:42).

Standing shoulder to shoulder in faith also means bearing one another's burdens (Galatians 6:2). The congregation becomes a network of spiritual interdependence, where no one fights alone. Even the most mature Christian requires the prayers, counsel, and companionship of others. This divine arrangement ensures that courage is renewed continually, for it flows not only from personal devotion but from the shared life of the body of Christ.

Mutual Edification and Accountability

Mutual edification lies at the core of Christian fellowship. The Apostle Paul wrote, "Let all things be done for building up" (1 Corinthians 14:26). Every gathering of believers, whether formal worship or personal interaction, is an opportunity to strengthen faith and holiness. Edification occurs when Scripture is taught accurately, when doctrine is upheld faithfully, and when love is expressed sincerely.

Accountability complements edification. True fellowship does not ignore sin or weakness but addresses them with truth and grace. Galatians 6:1 instructs, "Brothers, even if someone is caught in a trespass, you who are spiritual restore such a one in a spirit of gentleness." Such correction requires humility and courage. The goal is not condemnation but restoration — to bring a fellow believer back into full fellowship with Jehovah and His people.

Accountability also guards against complacency. When believers remind one another of their responsibilities and commitments, spiritual discipline is maintained. This mutual watchfulness strengthens courage because it eliminates the fear of isolation or failure. Each believer knows that others stand beside him, ready to guide and support him in the race of faith. In this way, the congregation functions as a living organism of truth and love, producing steadfast and mature disciples of Christ.

Protecting the Body from Fear and Division

The congregation must vigilantly guard against fear and division, for both are tools of the adversary. Fear paralyzes faith, and division erodes unity. In times of pressure or persecution, fear can spread like an infection, undermining courage. Yet 2 Timothy 1:7 reminds believers that "God did not give us a spirit of fear, but of power and love and soundness of mind." That power is exercised collectively when believers encourage one another to trust Jehovah's sovereignty.

Division often arises from pride, false teaching, or selfish ambition. The Apostle Paul warned the Corinthians against factions, urging them to "be perfectly united in mind and thought" (1 Corinthians 1:10). Protecting the body requires constant adherence to sound doctrine and humility among its members. Love binds believers together in perfect harmony (Colossians 3:14), but this love must be anchored in truth, not emotional sentiment.

A united congregation becomes a fortress of courage. When falsehood or fear attempts to infiltrate, the believers who are rooted in Scripture respond with discernment and steadfastness. Their fellowship serves as a protective wall, ensuring that faith remains strong and undivided. In such unity, courage thrives because believers know they are part of something eternal — the household of God, built on the foundation of the apostles and prophets, with Christ Jesus Himself as the cornerstone (Ephesians 2:20–22).

The Power of Shared Conviction

The courage that arises from fellowship is ultimately founded on shared conviction. This conviction is not opinion but a deeply held assurance grounded in the truth of God's Word. When believers share the same faith, purpose, and hope, their unity becomes unbreakable. The early Christians endured imprisonment, persecution, and even death because they stood together in the conviction that Christ had risen and that His Kingdom was certain.

Such shared conviction gives birth to courage that endures hardship and opposition. It transforms ordinary believers into witnesses of extraordinary faith. Acts 4:31 records that after the believers prayed together, "they were all filled with the Holy Spirit and began to speak the word of God with boldness." Their courage was the direct result of collective prayer and shared mission.

In every generation, the congregation remains the channel through which Jehovah strengthens His people. When believers assemble in unity, encourage one another in truth, and hold fast to their shared convictions, fear loses its grip. Courage becomes contagious, faith becomes visible, and love becomes active. The congregation thus reflects the divine design of mutual dependence — each believer strengthened by all, and all by Christ.

In this fellowship of faith, courage does not waver, for it is rooted in the eternal promises of God and fortified by the love of His people. The body of Christ stands unyielding amid the storms of the world, united in purpose, steadfast in hope,

FEARLESS

and fearless in service — because together, they have learned that courage through fellowship is one of Jehovah's greatest gifts to His congregation.

Edward D. Andrews

Chapter 13 – Fearless Leadership in the Church

Main Verse: "Shepherd the flock of God that is among you, exercising oversight, not under compulsion but willingly." — 1 Peter 5:2

The Call to Lead with Courage

The Church of Jesus Christ has always required leaders of courage, men who will not shrink back when faced with opposition, moral compromise, or doctrinal corruption. Peter's charge to shepherd the flock of God was not merely an exhortation to care for the people, but to do so with fearless conviction and faithful oversight. The elder or overseer (Greek *episkopos*) is not a position of status or prestige, but of responsibility before God. The shepherd must be vigilant, discerning, and steadfast, knowing that he answers not to the flock but to the Chief Shepherd, Jesus Christ Himself (1 Pet. 5:4).

Fearless leadership begins with a deep reverence for Jehovah and a complete trust in His inspired Word. The courage to lead does not come from human charisma or intellectual power but from the conviction that Scripture alone is sufficient and authoritative. When God appoints a man to shepherd His people, that man must accept the charge not under compulsion, but willingly, eagerly, and with humility. The fearless leader does not rely on public approval, nor does he bend to cultural trends that contradict God's truth. Rather, he stands immovable, anchored in Scripture, guarding the Church's purity and faithfulness.

True courage in leadership also demands a rejection of the fear of man. The apostle Paul wrote, "For am I now seeking the approval of man, or of God? ... If I were still trying to please man, I would not be a servant of Christ" (Gal. 1:10). The elder must measure every word, policy, and action by God's standard, not human sentiment. This requires moral fortitude, sound doctrine, and unwavering faith in the promises of God's Word. The fearless leader, therefore, does not lead to preserve his position or reputation but to fulfill a divine commission—to shepherd, to teach, to protect, and to model holiness.

Guarding the Flock Against False Teaching

In every generation, the Church has faced the intrusion of false teachers who twist Scripture for personal gain or worldly acceptance. The fearless leader must guard the flock with discernment, recognizing that error rarely announces itself openly but disguises itself in partial truths. Paul warned the Ephesian elders: "I know that after my departure fierce wolves will come in among you, not sparing the flock" (Acts 20:29). The faithful shepherd must therefore be alert, able to identify false doctrine, and ready to confront it with the sword of the Spirit—the Word of God.

False teachers undermine the authority of Scripture, question moral absolutes, and promote philosophies that gratify the flesh. Fearless leaders must expose such teachings and refute them publicly when necessary. This task demands deep study, prayer, and boldness. The shepherd must be "holding fast to the faithful word which is in accordance with the teaching, so that he will be able both to exhort in sound doctrine and to refute those who contradict" (Titus 1:9).

Guarding the flock also involves protecting the people from the subtle influence of worldly thinking. The modern Church is under immense pressure to accommodate secular ideologies, redefine marriage, and compromise on gender, morality, and truth. Fearless leaders must resist these corruptions, proclaiming that Scripture is not subject to reinterpretation according to culture. They must uphold the divine pattern of male leadership in the Church, the sanctity of marriage between one man and one woman, and the reality of moral accountability before a holy God.

The shepherd's vigilance is not merely defensive but proactive. He must train the congregation to be grounded in Scripture, equipping them to discern truth from error. This requires teaching with authority, consistency, and clarity, ensuring that every believer grows to maturity in Christ, "so that we may no longer be children, tossed to and fro by the waves and carried about by every wind of doctrine" (Eph. 4:14).

Integrity and Servant Leadership

Fearless leadership cannot exist apart from integrity. The spiritual leader's authority derives not from position or charisma but from his character. A leader who preaches holiness yet lives in hypocrisy destroys both his witness and his ministry. Integrity means alignment between belief, word, and action—a life wholly surrendered to Jehovah's will. Paul instructed Timothy that an overseer must be "above reproach, sober-minded, self-controlled, respectable, hospitable, able to teach" (1 Tim. 3:2).

Servant leadership is the heart of biblical authority. Jesus Christ, the ultimate Shepherd, "did not come to be served but to serve, and to give His life as a ransom for many" (Matt. 20:28). Fearless leaders emulate this model by leading not through domination but through humble service. Their leadership is marked by self-sacrifice, not self-promotion. They seek the spiritual welfare of others rather than personal gain. Peter warned against "shameful gain" and "lording it over those in your charge" (1 Pet. 5:2–3). Instead, the fearless leader willingly bears the burdens of others, offering guidance, comfort, and discipline in love.

Integrity also demands transparency and accountability. The elder must never manipulate, deceive, or conceal sin. He must model repentance, humility, and dependence on God's mercy. His life should be an open book, testifying to faithfulness in his marriage, purity in his conduct, and honesty in his dealings. The fearless leader knows that his authority is trustworthy only insofar as his life reflects the holiness of the One he represents.

Strength in Decision-Making and Discipline

Leadership requires the ability to make hard decisions grounded in biblical conviction rather than emotional preference. The shepherd must lead with clarity, wisdom, and firmness when matters of sin, doctrine, or order arise. Weak leadership avoids confrontation; fearless leadership addresses it in love and truth. When sin is tolerated, the Church's witness is compromised. When discipline is neglected, holiness is eroded.

Paul commanded the Corinthian congregation to remove unrepentant sinners from their midst (1 Cor. 5:13), not to punish them harshly but to preserve the purity of the Church and encourage repentance. The fearless leader understands that discipline is an act of love—a reflection of God's own fatherly correction (Heb. 12:6). Decision-making must always reflect God's revealed will, guided by Scripture and prayer.

Strength in leadership also involves unity and wisdom among a plurality of elders. Fearless leaders work together in harmony, balancing firmness with compassion, courage with grace. They do not act rashly or dictatorially but through collective discernment rooted in God's Word. When disagreement arises, they return to Scripture as the final authority, trusting that God's wisdom is sufficient to guide His Church.

Courageous Elders in an Apostate Age

We live in an age of widespread apostasy, where even many who claim the name of Christ reject the authority of the Bible, deny essential doctrines, and conform to the world's moral corruption. Fearless elders must stand as sentinels of truth in this spiritual darkness. They must not shrink back when culture mocks biblical teaching or when professing Christians compromise for popularity. They must proclaim with conviction that there is one faith, one Lord, one baptism, and one God and Father of all (Eph. 4:5–6).

The apostate age demands leaders who will not dilute the gospel. Many pulpits today are filled with those who preach self-esteem rather than repentance, prosperity rather than sanctification, and inclusivity rather than obedience. The fearless leader must boldly proclaim the narrow way that leads to life, even when few will walk it. He must remind the

Church that "friendship with the world is enmity with God" (Jas. 4:4). Such leaders may face rejection, ridicule, and even persecution, but they remain steadfast, knowing that faithfulness to Christ outweighs all temporal costs.

Jehovah has always preserved a remnant of faithful shepherds who refuse to bow to cultural idols or theological compromise. These men preach the whole counsel of God, even the hard truths about sin, judgment, and repentance. They resist the spirit of Antichrist that infiltrates the Church through deception and pride. Their courage is not human defiance but spiritual conviction—a confidence in God's sovereignty and the power of His Word.

Leading by Example and Endurance

The fearless leader's example is one of endurance under pressure. When the flock faces suffering, persecution, or confusion, the shepherd's steadfastness becomes a source of strength. His consistency in prayer, devotion, and faithfulness demonstrates that trust in God is not theoretical but lived out. Paul urged the Corinthians, "Be imitators of me, as I am of Christ" (1 Cor. 11:1). This pattern of imitation underscores that spiritual leadership is most effective when modeled rather than merely taught.

Endurance is essential because the path of leadership is often lonely and misunderstood. The elder will encounter criticism, betrayal, and seasons of weariness. Yet his perseverance is rooted in the eternal hope of Christ's return. Peter assures the faithful shepherds that "when the Chief Shepherd appears, you will receive the unfading crown of glory" (1 Pet. 5:4). This promise sustains the fearless leader through every hardship, reminding him that his labor is not in vain.

Leading by example also involves humility. The elder must never assume that leadership exempts him from service. He must be approachable, compassionate, and willing to admit his need for God's grace daily. His life must reflect the fruit of the Spirit—love, joy, peace, patience, kindness, goodness, faithfulness, gentleness, and self-control (Gal. 5:22–23). Through his example, the congregation learns what it means to walk faithfully before Jehovah.

Fearless leadership is not a product of natural temperament or human training but the work of God in a man who is wholly surrendered to His will. Such a leader is driven by love for the truth, love for the flock, and love for the Chief Shepherd. In an age of compromise, the Church desperately needs elders who will stand firm, guard the flock, and lead with integrity, courage, and faith.

Edward D. Andrews

Chapter 14 – Courage Through Suffering

Main Verse: *"Indeed, all who desire to live godly in Christ Jesus will be persecuted."* — 2 Timothy 3:12

Understanding the Source of Suffering

The question of suffering has challenged humanity since Eden. Why do people suffer? Is God to blame? The inspired Scriptures reveal that Jehovah did not design suffering as part of His original purpose for mankind. When Jehovah finished His creative works, He declared them "very good" (Genesis 1:31). This included the human pair, Adam and Eve, who were created perfect in body, mind, and moral capacity. They were not robots, but free moral agents with the ability to choose between obedience and disobedience. When they rebelled, they severed their relationship with God and introduced imperfection, pain, and death into human existence (Romans 5:12).

Thus, the Bible affirms that suffering was not part of Jehovah's purpose, nor does it originate from Him. James 1:13 emphatically declares: "When under trial, let no one say: 'I am being tried by God.' For with evil things God cannot be tried nor does He Himself try anyone." Jehovah does not bring about wickedness to test or punish people. Rather, humanity experiences the ongoing consequences of that first act of rebellion, combined with the personal misuse of free will throughout history.

Is God to Blame for Our Suffering?

Directly, no. Indirectly, yes. Jehovah is not the author of evil. Yet, as the Sovereign of the universe, He has allowed evil to continue temporarily for a purpose—to demonstrate once and for all the futility of independence from His rule. Suffering exists because Jehovah permits mankind to exercise free will without immediate intervention, so that His righteousness, wisdom, and justice might be vindicated when He ultimately restores peace through Christ's Kingdom.

Deuteronomy 32:4 proclaims, "All His ways are justice. A God of faithfulness who is never unjust." Likewise, Psalm 145:17 declares, "Jehovah is righteous in all His ways." These passages affirm His moral perfection. He cannot be the author of evil while also being the essence of righteousness.

However, Jehovah allows suffering as a consequence of human sin and imperfection. This permission, though painful for us, serves a purpose within His grand design: to show that humans cannot bring peace or happiness apart from His guidance. In time, His Kingdom will remove evil entirely and restore perfect conditions on earth.

Does God Cause Us to Suffer?

No. Jehovah never causes His faithful servants to suffer. As Job 34:12 states, "For a certainty, God does not act wickedly." The claim that God causes suffering or uses it to refine His people misrepresents His nature. Lamentations 3:38 makes this clear: "From the mouth of the Most High, bad things and what is good do not go forth."

Jehovah is holy and unchangeably good. He does not employ wickedness as an instrument of instruction or refinement. Many people mistakenly attribute their hardships to God, viewing them as divine tests of faith. But James 1:14-15 clarifies that these trials arise from internal desire: "Each one is tried by being drawn out and enticed by his own desire. Then the desire, when it has become fertile, gives birth to sin; in turn, sin, when it has been accomplished, brings forth death."

Jehovah's role is not to send trials but to provide strength to endure them. Through His Word and Spirit, He equips believers to remain steadfast despite the corruption and chaos of this world. He is our source of wisdom and endurance, never our source of distress (James 1:5; Philippians 4:13).

Is the Devil the Cause of All Suffering?

The Devil, though responsible for much evil, is not the cause of all suffering. Scripture calls him "the ruler of this world" (John 12:31) and "the wicked one" in whose power "the whole world is lying" (1 John 5:19). His rebellion corrupted human society and inspired disobedience against God. He seeks to "blind the minds of unbelievers" (2 Corinthians 4:4) and to promote moral decay.

Yet, not all suffering is directly caused by Satan's actions. Much arises from human imperfection and misuse of free will. Jehovah created mankind with the capacity to choose between right and wrong (Joshua 24:15). As Genesis 6:5 records, "Every inclination of the thoughts of the human heart was only evil all the time." Likewise, Genesis 8:21 states that "the inclination of man's heart is bad from his youth." These verses reveal that human sinfulness, combined with moral weakness, brings about countless forms of pain and injustice.

Galatians 6:7-8 reminds us that "whatever a man is sowing, this he will also reap." When humans make choices contrary to God's Word, they reap corruption and suffering—not because God decreed it, but because He has structured moral reality around cause and effect.

Does God Care About Our Suffering?

Yes. The Scriptures present Jehovah as deeply compassionate and aware of every tear His people shed. Isaiah 63:9 declares, "During all their distress it was distressing to Him." Jehovah is not indifferent to human pain. His concern is personal and tender. When the Israelites were enslaved in Egypt, He said, "I have certainly seen the affliction of My people... I well know the pains they suffer" (Exodus 3:7). His eyes are ever watchful, His heart empathetic (Psalm 56:8; 1 Peter 5:7).

Jehovah's compassion is not passive. He provides spiritual strength to endure suffering now and promises to eliminate it entirely in the future. Revelation 21:4 proclaims that He "will wipe out every tear from their eyes, and death will be no more, neither will mourning nor outcry nor pain be anymore." The resurrection hope (John 5:28-29) confirms that His care extends beyond the present life. He is not distant but intimately involved in the redemption and restoration of His people.

God Does Not Test Us

Jehovah does not use pain, loss, or disaster as instruments to refine His people. To claim otherwise is to attribute evil to Him. As James 1:13 makes clear, God cannot be tempted by evil, nor does He tempt anyone. Therefore, hardships are not divine experiments of faith. Rather, they are results of human sin, imperfection, and the conditions of a fallen world under Satan's influence.

Jehovah does allow hardship to continue temporarily but never for the purpose of inflicting pain or spiritual torment. He uses His inspired Word to train, correct, and guide—not to torment or test. The refining of faith occurs through obedience to Scripture and the exercise of endurance, not through inflicted suffering. Jehovah helps believers to mature spiritually through His truth, not through orchestrated trials (John 17:17).

Recognizing God's Overarching Purpose

Jehovah's plan encompasses more than our individual experiences. His purpose in allowing suffering is tied to the vindication of His sovereignty and the demonstration of the necessity of His righteous rule. Romans 8:28 teaches that "all things work together for good to those who love God," not because God manipulates every circumstance, but because His overarching plan will ultimately bring good from evil's temporary existence.

Throughout Scripture, faithful men and women endured suffering not as divine punishment but as evidence of their integrity amid a sinful world. Joseph suffered unjust imprisonment; Daniel faced persecution; the apostles endured beatings and imprisonment. In all these, Jehovah did not cause the suffering but sustained His servants through it.

Their endurance testified to the truth that only submission to God's sovereignty brings lasting peace.

In the present age, Jehovah continues to permit human society to experience the results of rejecting His authority, thereby teaching humanity the futility of independence. In due time, His Kingdom under Christ will rectify all injustice, proving beyond dispute that His rule is the only path to righteousness and peace.

Molinism: Navigating the Labyrinth of Foreknowledge and Free Will

The tension between divine foreknowledge and human freedom has long puzzled theologians. Molinism, named after Luis de Molina, provides a framework to understand how God's omniscience and human free will coexist. It introduces the idea of *middle knowledge* (scientia media)—God's knowledge of what free creatures would choose in any given circumstance.

This understanding aligns with Scripture's depiction of Jehovah as all-knowing (Psalm 147:5) yet never coercive. God's foreknowledge does not determine human actions. It is like observing a shadow before the substance appears; His knowledge reveals what will happen without causing it. Just as a barometer predicts weather without influencing it, Jehovah's omniscience reflects the outcomes of human choices without overriding their freedom.

Thus, Jehovah foreknew Adam's rebellion but did not cause it. His knowledge allowed for the provision of redemption through Christ before the foundation of the world (1 Peter 1:20). Divine foreknowledge ensures that Jehovah's purposes cannot fail, yet it never nullifies the free moral agency He granted to His intelligent creatures.

How Was It Possible for Adam to Sin If He Was Perfect?

Adam was created perfect (Genesis 1:27, 31). His perfection did not mean he was incapable of sin, but that he was morally complete, with no inherent tendency toward evil. Jehovah desired genuine love and obedience, which require freedom of choice (Deuteronomy 30:19-20; Joshua 24:15). If Adam had been programmed to obey automatically, he would have been a robot, not a moral being.

Perfection did not remove the capacity to sin; rather, it endowed Adam with the moral strength to choose rightly. His sin resulted from the willful indulgence of wrong desire. James 1:14-15 explains, "Each one is tried by being drawn out and enticed by his own desire. Then the desire, when it has become fertile, gives birth to sin." When Eve entertained Satan's lies and Adam yielded to her persuasion, both allowed wrong thoughts to develop into sinful action (Genesis 3:1-6).

Their sin did not arise from a flaw in creation but from the misuse of freedom. Perfection includes the ability to choose righteousness out of love, not compulsion. Adam's choice to sin was not inevitable; it was a voluntary act of rebellion. By contrast, Christ, the "last Adam," remained obedient even unto death (1 Corinthians 15:45; Philippians

2:8), proving that perfect humanity can remain loyal under trial.

Courage Through Suffering

The Apostle Paul's words in 2 Timothy 3:12 remind all true Christians that "all who desire to live godly in Christ Jesus will be persecuted." Courage through suffering arises from faith in Jehovah's justice, confidence in His purpose, and hope in His promises. Jehovah does not cause suffering, but He strengthens His servants to endure it faithfully.

Christians are not exempt from pain, yet their suffering is transformed by perspective. They see beyond the immediate hardship to the greater purpose—the vindication of God's sovereignty and the assurance of His Kingdom's triumph. When believers suffer, they imitate Christ, who "suffered for righteousness' sake" and "entrusted Himself to Him who judges righteously" (1 Peter 2:19-23).

True courage comes not from denying suffering, but from trusting Jehovah's goodness amidst it. Though He allows evil temporarily, His purpose remains steadfast: to redeem, restore, and ultimately remove all suffering through the reign of His Son, Jesus Christ. Until then, those who live godly in Christ must bear their trials with faith, hope, and courage, knowing that their endurance glorifies Jehovah and anticipates the day when "the former things will not be called to mind" (Isaiah 65:17).

Chapter 15 – Courage to Forgive

Main Verse: *"Be kind to one another, tenderhearted, forgiving one another, just as God also in Christ forgave you."* — Ephesians 4:32

Forgiveness as an Act of Strength

Forgiveness is not weakness, nor is it the passive surrender of one's rights. It is, rather, the highest expression of moral strength and spiritual maturity. To forgive is to imitate the very nature of God, Who is "compassionate and gracious, slow to anger, and abundant in loyal love" (Psalm 103:8). The Christian life is not one of self-exaltation or pride but of humility and Christlike love that reflects Jehovah's forgiving character.

Many perceive forgiveness as condoning wrongdoing or allowing injustice to go unanswered. Yet true forgiveness does not nullify righteousness or dismiss accountability. It acknowledges the wrong, understands the pain it has caused, and still releases the offender from the debt of vengeance. The one who forgives relinquishes personal retaliation and entrusts justice to Jehovah, Who "will by no means leave the guilty unpunished" (Exodus 34:7). This requires courage because it means surrendering one's desire for retribution and trusting in God's perfect judgment.

Forgiveness demonstrates spiritual strength because it demands the mastery of one's emotions. It means overcoming pride, hurt, and resentment through the power of a renewed mind. As the apostle Paul admonished, "Do not be overcome by evil, but overcome evil with good" (Romans 12:21). The believer who forgives exercises dominion over anger and bitterness, thus proving that the Spirit-inspired Word has transformed the heart.

Breaking the Chains of Bitterness

Bitterness is the poisonous root that grows in the heart of the unforgiving. It corrodes peace, steals joy, and poisons relationships. Hebrews 12:15 warns, "See to it that no one falls short of the grace of God and that no root of bitterness springs up, causing trouble and defiling many." Bitterness enslaves both the one who harbors it and those within his or her influence.

The person who refuses to forgive becomes a prisoner of past offenses. Each recollection of injury fuels resentment, trapping the mind in continual suffering. Forgiveness, therefore, is liberation. It breaks the spiritual bondage that bitterness creates. It restores fellowship with God, for Jesus taught that our forgiveness from the Father is linked to our willingness to forgive others: "For if you forgive people their offenses, your heavenly Father will also forgive you; but if you do not forgive people, neither will your Father forgive your offenses" (Matthew 6:14–15).

Bitterness blinds the soul to grace. It causes one to dwell in the darkness of self-pity rather than in the light of God's mercy. When believers forgive, they uproot the seeds of resentment before they take hold. This requires courage, for it is often easier to dwell upon injustice than to release it. Yet the act of forgiveness transforms bitterness into blessing and allows peace to take root in the heart.

The Example of Christ's Forgiveness

The supreme model of forgiveness is Jesus Christ. While being nailed to the stake, enduring agony and humiliation, He uttered the words that reveal the very heart of divine mercy: "Father, forgive them, for they do not know what they are doing" (Luke 23:34). His plea was not conditional, nor did it depend upon the immediate repentance of His persecutors. It flowed from a heart perfectly aligned with Jehovah's will — a heart filled with compassion, grace, and truth.

Christ's forgiveness was courageous because it was given amidst suffering. He did not wait for justice to be served before showing mercy. His forgiveness was proactive, not reactive. It revealed that true strength is not expressed through retaliation but through love that conquers hate. When believers forgive, they walk in the footsteps of Christ, manifesting the same self-sacrificial love that defined His earthly ministry.

Paul exhorts Christians to imitate this pattern: "Just as the Lord forgave you, so also should you" (Colossians 3:13). The believer who remembers the depth of Christ's mercy can never justify withholding forgiveness from another. We have been forgiven an unpayable debt; therefore, to refuse forgiveness is to forget the grace we ourselves have received. The courage to forgive others springs from gratitude for what Jehovah has done through Christ.

Courage to Let Go of Wrongs

To forgive is to let go — not of justice or truth, but of personal vengeance and the desire to inflict equal pain. Letting go is not amnesia; it is a conscious decision to release the emotional claim we hold against another person. It is a deliberate act of the will, enabled by obedience to Scripture and the humility that flows from faith.

Forgiveness does not minimize wrongdoing but recognizes that Jehovah alone has the authority to judge rightly. Romans 12:19 declares, "Beloved, never avenge yourselves, but leave room for the wrath of God, for it is written, 'Vengeance is Mine, I will repay,' says Jehovah." This acknowledgment frees the believer from the exhausting burden of revenge and allows one to experience the tranquility that comes from trusting in God's justice.

Letting go of wrongs requires courage because the flesh naturally desires vindication. Yet through prayer and meditation upon God's Word, the believer gains the strength to surrender these feelings to Jehovah. When we release grudges, we create space for peace, healing, and restoration to enter. In doing so, we reflect the heart of God, Who chooses to "remember sins no more" (Hebrews 8:12).

Love That Overcomes Resentment

True forgiveness flows from love — not sentimental affection, but the selfless, active love that seeks the good of others despite their failures. The Greek term *agapē* describes a love grounded in principle, not emotion. It is the kind of love that Jesus demonstrated toward His disciples, who often failed Him, yet whom He continued to guide, protect, and restore.

Paul captures this divine love in 1 Corinthians 13:5 when he says that love "does not take into account a wrong suffered." The one who forgives through love refuses to keep a record of offenses. Love transforms resentment into compassion and anger into understanding. It is not blind to wrongdoing but chooses to overcome it by doing good.

The courage to forgive springs from a heart filled with this *agapē* love. When love governs the believer's response, resentment cannot survive. Such love is not humanly generated; it is the product of God's Word working powerfully in the heart. The apostle John reminds us that "we love because He first loved us" (1 John 4:19). When the Christian contemplates the immeasurable love Jehovah has shown through Christ, the bitterness that once ruled the heart begins to dissolve. Love that forgives reflects divine mercy and brings reconciliation where hatred once divided.

Healing and Restoration Through Forgiveness

Forgiveness brings healing not only to relationships but also to the soul of the forgiver. Unforgiveness festers into spiritual decay, affecting one's prayer life, worship, and fellowship. It clouds judgment and disrupts peace. Yet when forgiveness is extended, restoration begins. Psalm 147:3 declares, "He heals the brokenhearted and binds up their wounds." The believer who forgives experiences this healing because forgiveness aligns the heart with God's purposes.

Restoration is the fruit of genuine forgiveness. When believers reconcile through humility and repentance, they reflect the unity that Christ prayed for in John 17:21 — "that they may all be one." Forgiveness restores harmony in the body of Christ, strengthens the testimony of the congregation, and glorifies Jehovah, Who is the source of all reconciliation.

Moreover, forgiveness renews personal joy. The believer who chooses mercy over resentment experiences the peace that "surpasses all understanding" (Philippians 4:7). Forgiveness is the divine remedy for human conflict, the bridge that spans the gap between offense and grace. It demonstrates that God's love is stronger than sin, His mercy deeper than pain, and His purpose greater than our failures.

Thus, the courage to forgive is not merely a moral virtue — it is the evidence of divine transformation. It reveals that Christ's life is being reproduced within the believer. To forgive is to participate in the redemptive work of God, bringing light where darkness once prevailed and life where resentment once reigned.

Edward D. Andrews

Chapter 16 – Courage in Waiting for Jehovah

Main Verse: *"Wait for Jehovah; be strong, and let your heart take courage; wait for Jehovah!"* — Psalm 27:14

The Strength Found in Patience

Patience is not passive resignation, but the active endurance of faith that clings to Jehovah in expectation of His deliverance. The psalmist David, in the midst of peril and uncertainty, could say with unwavering conviction, "Wait for Jehovah." This call to patience arises not from human calmness but from divine confidence. The one who waits on Jehovah demonstrates trust in His wisdom and timing rather than his own understanding.

True patience is spiritual strength under pressure. It is the steadfast refusal to allow circumstances, fear, or despair to dictate the heart's direction. It is spiritual maturity refined through adversity, teaching the believer to depend fully upon the faithfulness of Jehovah. The one who waits is not idle but watchful, alert, and submissive to divine purpose.

When a Christian cultivates patience, he participates in the process of sanctification, learning to endure with courage. James 1:4 urges, "Let endurance have its full effect, that you may be complete and whole, lacking in nothing." This completeness comes only when faith is tested and proves genuine. Waiting, therefore, is not weakness; it is the measure of one's confidence in God's unchanging promises.

The patient believer rests upon Jehovah's reliability. He does not seek shortcuts, nor does he surrender to despair when delays come. Instead, he strengthens his heart with the knowledge that every promise of God will come to pass in its appointed time.

Trusting in God's Perfect Timing

Jehovah's timing is flawless, though it often contrasts sharply with human expectation. Scripture repeatedly reminds us that the Creator's schedule is guided by His omniscient purpose, not by our impatience. "For My thoughts are not your thoughts, nor are your ways My ways," declares Jehovah through Isaiah (Isaiah 55:8).

When Abraham awaited the promised son, years passed before Isaac was born. When Joseph languished in prison, it was years before he saw deliverance and purpose in his suffering. When Israel groaned under Egyptian oppression, Jehovah waited until "the fullness of time" to raise Moses. When the world awaited redemption, "at the right time Christ died for the ungodly" (Romans 5:6).

In every case, divine timing fulfilled divine intention. What may appear as delay to human perception is, in reality, the perfect orchestration of Jehovah's plan. To trust Him in waiting is to acknowledge His sovereignty over time and circumstance.

The believer must learn to surrender the demand for immediate results. Impatience reveals a heart that desires control, while faith rests in the certainty that Jehovah's purposes will never fail. Trusting in His timing means relinquishing anxiety and embracing peace. The path of the righteous is illuminated not by how swiftly he moves, but by how faithfully he waits.

To wait with courage is to live in daily submission to God's order of events. It is a declaration of faith that His plan, though unseen, is unfolding precisely as He wills.

Enduring Delays Without Fear

Delays often produce fear — fear that God has forgotten, that He has turned away, or that His promises will remain unfulfilled. Yet such fears arise from misunderstanding Jehovah's nature. He does not abandon His people, nor does He forget His covenant. David wrote, "I would have despaired unless I had believed that I would see the goodness of Jehovah in the land of the living" (Psalm 27:13).

Courage in delay is not found in self-assurance, but in divine assurance. The believer endures delays without fear because he knows Jehovah is near, even when unseen. His silence does not indicate absence; it often indicates preparation. During those quiet seasons, God is aligning circumstances, refining character, and deepening dependence.

Fear thrives where faith wanes. Thus, courage must be cultivated through remembrance of God's past faithfulness. The one who recalls how Jehovah has delivered before will not faint when He seems to delay again. The stories of Scripture are testimonies of divine reliability — Elijah's sustenance in drought, Daniel's protection in the lions' den, and Paul's endurance amid persecution — all reveal the faithfulness of God who acts at the right moment.

Faithful endurance is the antidote to fear. It transforms waiting from a season of anxiety into a season of spiritual strengthening. As Isaiah wrote, "Those who wait for Jehovah will gain new strength; they will mount up with wings like eagles; they will run and not get tired; they will walk and not become weary" (Isaiah 40:31). The waiting soul discovers that what appears to be delay is actually divine preparation for renewal.

Faith That Waits Without Fainting

Faith that waits without fainting is the faith that truly knows Jehovah. It is the conviction that He is as good in the waiting as He is in the fulfilling. Many faint because they focus on what is withheld rather than on Who sustains them. True faith, however, lifts its gaze beyond the moment and anchors itself in the eternal reliability of God's Word.

When Jesus delayed His arrival at Bethany after hearing of Lazarus' sickness, it was not indifference but purpose. He declared, "This sickness is not to end in death, but for the glory of God" (John 11:4). The delay magnified the miracle, revealing the glory of Christ in resurrection power. Thus, what seemed like neglect was divine intention.

The believer must therefore interpret delay through the lens of faith, not frustration. Waiting is not the absence of God's work but the arena in which He performs His deepest transformations. It is in the waiting that endurance is perfected, pride is humbled, and hope is purified.

Faith that refuses to faint draws life from Scripture, prayer, and remembrance. It feeds on divine promises and rejects the temptation to give up. As Hebrews 10:36 reminds, "You have need of endurance, so that when you have done the will of God, you may receive what was promised."

Jehovah never fails to fulfill His Word, but He fulfills it in the fullness of His wisdom. Faith that endures learns to rejoice not merely in the outcome but in the sanctifying process of waiting itself.

The Peace of Resting in God's Will

Resting in God's will is the highest expression of trust. It is not resignation, but the calm assurance that His plan is always best. When one truly rests in Jehovah, peace replaces panic, and confidence replaces confusion. "Commit your way to Jehovah; trust in Him, and He will act" (Psalm 37:5).

Rest is not inactivity; it is inward stability grounded in the certainty of divine care. The peace that comes from resting in God's will is a peace beyond comprehension (Philippians 4:7), guarding the heart and mind from anxiety. The one who waits courageously experiences tranquility amid turmoil because his confidence lies not in changeable circumstances but in the unchanging character of God.

The peace of resting in Jehovah also frees the believer from comparison and complaint. It allows him to walk faithfully in the present without envying those who seem to move ahead. Every soul's journey unfolds according to God's unique design, and the one who trusts His hand will not fret over the pace of progress.

Resting in God's will means embracing each moment as ordained by His wisdom. The believer no longer measures success by speed but by obedience. In this peace, courage thrives, and faith is fortified.

Learning Dependence Through Waiting

Waiting is one of God's most effective means of teaching dependence. It strips away self-sufficiency and compels the believer to cling to divine strength. When human ability is exhausted, and all plans falter, the soul learns that Jehovah alone sustains.

Moses waited forty years in Midian before leading Israel. David waited years after his anointing before ascending the throne. Paul spent time in obscurity before beginning his missionary work. In every case, waiting was preparation — a divine classroom in which humility, patience, and reliance were taught.

Dependence learned through waiting is not weakness but wisdom. It acknowledges that every blessing flows from God's hand and that without Him, nothing endures. As Proverbs 3:5-6 exhorts, "Trust in Jehovah with all your heart and do not lean on your own understanding. In all your ways acknowledge Him, and He will make your paths straight."

The one who waits learns to listen more carefully, pray more fervently, and obey more fully. He discovers that true strength is not independence but surrender. Jehovah allows seasons of delay not to discourage His servants, but to deepen their trust and refine their devotion.

When the believer emerges from waiting, he does so with greater spiritual maturity and clearer vision. His courage is no longer drawn from personal determination but from divine sufficiency. He has learned that the waiting was not wasted — it was sanctified time, shaping his heart to mirror the patience and faithfulness of God Himself.

Edward D. Andrews

Chapter 17 – Fearless Evangelism in a Decaying World

Main Verse: *"Go therefore and make disciples of all nations."* — Matthew 28:19

Courage to Proclaim Christ Boldly

In a world that continually descends into moral decay, Christians are called to stand as fearless witnesses of Jesus Christ. The Great Commission is not an optional endeavor for the few who feel gifted in public speaking or ministry work; it is the divine command of the risen Christ to every follower of His. When Jesus said, "Go therefore and make disciples of all nations," He established evangelism as the heartbeat of the Christian life. To obey this command requires unshakable courage, not born of human confidence but of trust in Jehovah's power and presence.

The first-century disciples faced persecution, imprisonment, and even death for proclaiming Christ. Yet, empowered by the Holy Spirit's direction through Scripture, they boldly declared that "there is salvation in no one else" (Acts 4:12). This same divine courage must characterize the modern believer. The Christian's authority to proclaim the message does not rest in worldly credentials but in the truth of the Gospel and the command of Christ Himself. True courage in evangelism begins when one fears Jehovah more than man, when the desire to please God outweighs the dread of human rejection.

To proclaim Christ boldly, believers must anchor themselves in the conviction that God's Word is the ultimate and absolute truth. In an age of relativism, where truth is treated as a matter of personal preference, evangelism demands clarity, not compromise. The message of salvation through Jesus Christ must be presented without dilution or apology, regardless of whether the hearer welcomes or rejects it.

Evangelism as a Test of Faith

Evangelism serves as a powerful measure of one's faith in God's promises. It exposes whether we truly believe that the Gospel is the power of God for salvation (Romans 1:16). When a believer hesitates to share the good news due to fear, self-consciousness, or the anticipation of ridicule, it reveals a struggle between faith and flesh. True faith acts. It trusts that

Jehovah will provide the strength, the words, and the opportunity to reach receptive hearts.

The early Christians did not wait for favorable conditions before proclaiming Christ. They evangelized in marketplaces, synagogues, homes, and even prisons. Paul, while chained for the Gospel, wrote that "the word of God is not bound" (2 Timothy 2:9). This same unbreakable confidence must define every modern disciple. Evangelism tests the authenticity of one's belief in Christ's authority and His power to draw all men to Himself.

Faithful evangelism also tests the believer's submission to Scripture. The Word commands, "Always be ready to make a defense to everyone who asks you to give an account for the hope that is in you" (1 Peter 3:15). A silent Christian contradicts the very purpose of salvation, which is to glorify Christ through word and deed. To withhold the message of life from those perishing in spiritual darkness is an act of spiritual negligence.

Standing Firm in the Great Commission

To stand firm in the Great Commission is to remain steadfast in obedience to Christ's command, regardless of cultural pressures or political climates. The Church today faces increasing hostility, not only from atheistic ideologies but also from compromised religious systems that dilute the truth for social acceptance. Yet, the command remains unchanged. Christ's followers are to make disciples of all nations, baptizing them and teaching them to observe everything He commanded.

Standing firm requires endurance. The Christian must not be distracted by the temporary allure of comfort or the deceptive message of tolerance that demands silence on matters of sin and righteousness. Jesus warned that the world would hate His followers because it first hated Him (John 15:18–20). Therefore, faithfulness to the Great Commission involves perseverance through misunderstanding, rejection, and sometimes persecution.

Every believer must remember that the authority behind the Great Commission rests on Christ's universal sovereignty. Before giving the command to "go," Jesus declared, "All authority in heaven and on earth has been given to Me" (Matthew 28:18). This assurance guarantees that no earthly power can hinder God's redemptive plan. When Christians carry the Gospel message, they go under divine authority, protected and directed by Christ Himself.

Overcoming Rejection and Hostility

Rejection is an inevitable aspect of evangelism in a world corrupted by sin. When Christians share the Gospel, they confront hearts hardened by pride and blinded by Satan (2 Corinthians 4:4). Yet, believers must remember that rejection of the message is not a rejection of the messenger but of Christ Himself. Jesus said, "If they reject you, they are rejecting Me" (Luke 10:16).

The fear of rejection often silences many well-intentioned believers. However, Scripture reminds us that the approval of men is fleeting, but the approval of Jehovah endures forever. When Paul faced ridicule and persecution, he declared, "I am not seeking the approval of man, but of God" (Galatians 1:10). This mindset empowers Christians to press forward even when their message is met with hostility.

Hostility toward the Gospel is not new. The prophets were mocked, imprisoned, and even killed for speaking Jehovah's truth. Jesus Himself was despised and rejected, yet He remained faithful to His mission. Likewise, those who follow Him must endure opposition without bitterness. The Christian response to hostility must reflect the meekness and love of Christ, who prayed for those who crucified Him. By displaying such spiritual strength, believers demonstrate that their confidence lies not in human approval but in divine purpose.

Overcoming rejection also requires wisdom. Jesus instructed His disciples to be "wise as serpents and innocent as doves" (Matthew 10:16). This means speaking truth with discernment and gentleness, recognizing when to persist and when to move on. Evangelism is not about winning arguments but about faithfully presenting truth with love, allowing Jehovah to work in the hearts of the hearers.

Speaking Truth in a World That Rejects It

The modern world increasingly labels biblical truth as intolerance. Absolute moral standards are ridiculed, sin is celebrated, and righteousness is dismissed as outdated. Yet, the Christian is called to proclaim truth regardless of societal approval. The Gospel exposes sin, convicts the heart, and calls for repentance—a message that naturally offends the proud but liberates the humble.

Jesus declared, "You will know the truth, and the truth will make you free" (John 8:32). This truth liberates men and women from the bondage of sin and death, leading them to eternal life through faith in Christ. However, for this truth to transform, it must first be spoken. Silence in the face of error is complicity with darkness. Therefore, Christians must lovingly yet firmly speak the truths of Scripture even when such truth contradicts the values of modern culture.

Speaking truth courageously requires that believers remain grounded in Scripture. The Bible alone defines righteousness, salvation, and moral order. When Christians compromise biblical teaching to accommodate cultural trends, they betray the trust placed upon them as ambassadors of Christ. The Apostle Paul warned against those who would "distort the gospel of Christ" (Galatians 1:7). A fearless evangelist must speak what God has spoken, without alteration or omission.

Furthermore, speaking truth in a rejecting world must be done with compassion. Jesus did not preach condemnation without extending mercy. He offered forgiveness to those willing to repent. The Christian message must always balance truth with grace—confronting sin while pointing to the Savior who offers redemption.

Eternal Rewards for the Faithful Witness

Every act of faithful evangelism is seen and remembered by Jehovah. Jesus promised, "Whoever acknowledges Me before men, I will also acknowledge before My Father in heaven" (Matthew 10:32). The eternal reward for courageous proclamation far outweighs any temporary suffering endured for Christ's sake.

The faithful evangelist participates in the very work of God's Kingdom. Each soul won for Christ adds to the eternal glory of Jehovah. The Apostle Paul described those he led to faith as his "joy and crown" in the presence of the Lord (1 Thessalonians 2:19). The believer who endures ridicule, rejection, or hardship for the Gospel will receive an imperishable reward—eternal life in the restored earth under Christ's righteous reign.

Even when results seem unseen, the faithful witness can rest in the assurance that God's Word never returns empty (Isaiah 55:11). Every testimony, every Scripture shared, every act of love motivated by faith plants a seed that Jehovah can cause to grow in His time. The Christian's duty is not to convert but to proclaim; the results belong to God.

In the coming Kingdom, those who have labored in evangelism will rejoice as they see the fruits of their work—people from every nation and tongue redeemed through the message of Christ. This eternal perspective strengthens the believer to endure present hostility, knowing that the final reward is everlasting joy in the service of the King of Kings.

Edward D. Andrews

Chapter 18 – Courage in Spiritual Warfare

Main Verse: *"Be strong in the Lord and in the strength of his might."* — Ephesians 6:10

Recognizing the Invisible Battle

The Christian life unfolds within a realm far greater than what physical eyes can perceive. Scripture reveals that believers are engaged in a vast, invisible conflict between righteousness and wickedness, between the kingdom of God and the dominion of Satan. The Apostle Paul, writing to the Ephesians, lifts the veil from this unseen arena, declaring that "our struggle is not against blood and flesh, but against the rulers, against the authorities, against the world rulers of this darkness, against the wicked spirit forces in the heavenly places" (Ephesians 6:12). This is not a symbolic description; it is a literal portrayal of the spiritual war that has persisted since the rebellion of Satan and his demons against Jehovah.

Every Christian, by virtue of allegiance to Christ, has entered this battleground. The conflict is not fought with physical weapons nor resolved through human reasoning or diplomacy. It is spiritual warfare waged through faith, truth, and obedience to God's Word. Satan, "the god of this system of things" (2 Corinthians 4:4), orchestrates deception, temptation, and persecution to weaken and destroy faith. Yet Jehovah has not left His people defenseless. Through His inspired Word and the indwelling power of His might—not within us, but operative through His Spirit-inspired Scripture—He equips believers to withstand the enemy's schemes.

This recognition of the unseen battle is essential. To ignore it is to walk unarmed into combat. The believer who grasps the reality of this warfare does not attribute difficulties merely to coincidence or human opposition, but understands that behind these pressures lies a spiritual enemy seeking to devour (1 Peter 5:8). Therefore, courage begins with awareness. Knowing that the struggle is spiritual, the Christian must prepare spiritually, relying wholly on Jehovah's strength and direction.

The Weapons of Righteousness

Paul describes the spiritual armor in Ephesians 6:13–17 with vivid imagery drawn from the Roman soldier's battle gear. Each piece represents a divine provision for the believer's defense and offense in spiritual warfare. These are not optional accessories; they form a complete system of spiritual fortification.

The belt of truth girds the mind and heart, enabling the believer to move freely and decisively in the service of God. Truth is not subjective or emotional but grounded in the unchanging revelation of Scripture. The breastplate of righteousness protects the heart—the center of moral and spiritual life—from the accusations and corruption of sin. This righteousness is not self-generated but imputed through faith in Christ and maintained by living in harmony with God's commands.

The sandals of readiness represent a willingness to proclaim the good news of peace. The Christian stands firm and moves forward, stabilized by the message of reconciliation that brings peace between God and man through Christ. The shield of faith, broad and mobile, extinguishes all the flaming arrows of the wicked one—doubts, fears, slanders, and seductions. Faith acts as a dynamic defense, deflecting every attack by trusting in Jehovah's promises and power.

The helmet of salvation guards the mind against despair and confusion. Assurance of salvation provides mental clarity and confidence in the face of adversity. Finally, the sword of the Spirit, which is the Word of God, serves as the only offensive weapon. It is sharper than any double-edged sword (Hebrews 4:12), cutting through deception and exposing the truth. The Christian who wields this weapon skillfully through knowledge and application of Scripture can repel temptation, correct error, and proclaim the authority of God.

These weapons of righteousness are sufficient for every battle because they come from Jehovah Himself. The believer's task is not to invent new strategies but to faithfully use the divine armor provided. Spiritual courage flows from confidence in these heavenly resources, not in personal strength or cleverness.

Standing Firm Against the Evil One

Courage in spiritual warfare manifests most clearly in steadfastness. Paul exhorts believers to "stand firm" (Ephesians 6:13–14), a command that implies perseverance under pressure rather than aggression for personal gain. To stand firm is to hold one's ground when Satan assaults through deception, temptation, or persecution. This courage is not passive endurance but active faithfulness.

The Evil One thrives on intimidation. He seeks to induce fear, compromise, or discouragement. But Jehovah commands His people to "resist him, firm in the faith" (1 Peter 5:9). Resistance is not a single act but a continual stance of loyalty to God's truth. The believer stands firm by rejecting worldly ideologies, false teachings, and moral corruption. Each act of obedience weakens the enemy's influence and strengthens the believer's resolve.

To stand firm also means refusing to retreat when obedience is costly. Whether faced with ridicule, loss, or persecution, the faithful Christian remembers that Christ

Himself endured hostility and triumphed (John 16:33). Courage in battle arises from identification with Christ's victory. As Paul proclaimed, "Thanks be to God, who always leads us in triumph in Christ" (2 Corinthians 2:14). Therefore, spiritual steadfastness is not rooted in human resilience but in divine assurance. The believer knows that Jehovah's power sustains him and that no force of darkness can separate him from God's love (Romans 8:38–39).

Prayer and the Word as Defense

No soldier can endure long in battle without communication and sustenance. In spiritual warfare, prayer and the Word of God fulfill these vital roles. Paul concludes his discussion of the armor by commanding believers to be "praying at all times in spirit, with every form of prayer and supplication" (Ephesians 6:18). Prayer keeps the Christian in continual contact with Jehovah, seeking His wisdom, strength, and guidance.

True prayer in spiritual warfare is not ritualistic or formulaic. It is heartfelt communication rooted in dependence. Through prayer, believers acknowledge their insufficiency and Jehovah's supremacy. Courage is renewed in the awareness that the Almighty hears and answers. As Jesus instructed His followers, they must "always pray and not give up" (Luke 18:1). Persistent prayer fortifies faith and opens the heart to divine reinforcement.

The Word of God, meanwhile, serves both as instruction and defense. When Satan tempted Jesus in the wilderness, Christ repelled every assault with the authoritative declaration, "It is written" (Matthew 4:1–11). Each citation from Scripture cut through the deception, affirming the supremacy of divine truth. Likewise, the Christian who studies, memorizes, and applies Scripture is equipped to discern and defeat spiritual lies. The Word is not merely a source of comfort but a weapon that pierces the enemy's strategy.

Together, prayer and Scripture form a dual line of defense. Prayer keeps the believer connected to the Commander, and the Word provides the strategy for battle. When both are active, courage thrives, for the Christian fights not in isolation but in communion with Jehovah and armed with His unerring truth.

Perseverance in the Face of Opposition

Spiritual warfare demands endurance. The battle does not end quickly, nor does the enemy relent. Satan's assaults may vary in intensity and method, but his goal remains the same—to erode faith and silence the testimony of God's people. Thus, perseverance is both a necessity and a demonstration of spiritual courage.

James writes, "Blessed is the man who remains steadfast under trial, for once he has been approved, he will receive the crown of life which Jehovah has promised to those who love Him" (James 1:12). Perseverance is not stoic survival; it is continued faithfulness grounded in love for God. The believer who endures does so not because the struggle is easy but because he trusts Jehovah's promises and hopes in His deliverance.

Perseverance also involves maintaining integrity amid hostility. When pressures mount, the temptation arises to compromise truth or moral standards for temporary relief. Yet Jesus declared, "The one who has endured to the end will be saved" (Matthew 24:13). Such endurance is evidence of genuine faith and loyalty. It reflects an unwavering conviction that God's purposes will prevail and that no opposition, however fierce, can thwart His plan.

This courage is exemplified by countless believers throughout history who faced persecution with unyielding faith. From the early Christians in Rome to faithful witnesses in every age, their perseverance stands as testimony to Jehovah's sustaining power. The same God who upheld them strengthens His people today through His Word, enabling them to press forward with hope and courage.

Triumph in Jehovah's Strength

Victory in spiritual warfare belongs not to human might but to divine power. Paul's exhortation, "Be strong in the Lord and in the strength of his might" (Ephesians 6:10), reminds believers that the source of all spiritual courage and triumph is Jehovah Himself. The Christian's role is not to manufacture strength but to draw upon the inexhaustible reservoir of divine power available through faith and obedience.

Jehovah's strength is demonstrated most vividly in human weakness. As Paul declared, "When I am weak, then I am strong" (2 Corinthians 12:10). This paradox expresses the essence of spiritual courage. When the believer acknowledges dependence on God, divine strength becomes operative. The power that raised Christ from the dead works in those who believe (Ephesians 1:19–20). This power does not merely help believers survive spiritual conflict—it ensures ultimate victory.

The triumph of Jehovah's strength is also eschatological. Christ's victory at His resurrection guarantees the final overthrow of Satan and the complete establishment of God's Kingdom. Those who remain faithful share in that victory, not as spectators but as participants. Revelation 12:11 declares, "They conquered him because of the blood of the Lamb and because of the word of their testimony." Courage in spiritual warfare therefore looks forward to this assured outcome. The believer fights not in uncertainty but in confidence that the final victory is already secured through Christ.

To live courageously in spiritual warfare is to walk daily in Jehovah's strength, clothed with His armor, guided by His Word, and sustained by prayer. It is to stand firm against every assault of the enemy, persevering in faith and hope until the day when the warfare ends, and the faithful enter eternal peace under the rule of Christ.

Edward D. Andrews

Chapter 19 – Courage in the Face of Apostasy

Main Verse: *"For the time will come when they will not endure sound doctrine."* — 2 Timothy 4:3

Identifying the Great Falling Away

The apostle Paul's warning to Timothy is one of the most sobering prophecies concerning the end times of the Christian congregation. The phrase "the time will come when they will not endure sound doctrine" (2 Timothy 4:3) reveals both a forecast and a call to vigilance. The "great falling away," or apostasy, was foretold to occur within the very framework of professed Christianity, not from without. This apostasy would not begin as an external persecution but as an internal corruption of teaching, faith, and conduct.

Paul had already written earlier to the Thessalonians, saying, "Let no one deceive you in any way. For that day will not come, unless the apostasy comes first" (2 Thessalonians 2:3). Apostasy means a deliberate departure from the truth, not a mere misunderstanding. It is a conscious abandonment of the faith once delivered to the holy ones (Jude 3). Historically, this falling away began within the first few centuries after the apostles' deaths, when human traditions, philosophical speculations, and hierarchical structures began to replace the pure teaching of Scripture. Pagan rituals were baptized into Christian form, and the simplicity of apostolic worship was exchanged for ritualism and clerical power.

The apostasy continues today under many guises—denominations that deny the inspiration and authority of Scripture, churches that replace repentance with self-esteem, and teachers who proclaim a "gospel" of prosperity instead of the message of salvation through faith and obedience to Christ. The same pattern that Paul identified—people "accumulating teachers to suit their own passions" (2 Timothy 4:3)—defines the religious marketplace of our age. The danger lies not in persecution from unbelievers, but in seduction by those who claim to speak for Christ while undermining His Word.

Remaining Faithful to Sound Doctrine

Sound doctrine is not the invention of theologians or traditions; it is the faithful teaching of what the inspired Scriptures declare. The Greek word translated "sound" (hygiainō) means "healthy" or "wholesome." Just as the body requires nourishment, the believer's faith must be sustained by healthy teaching that aligns with the full counsel of God.

Paul repeatedly exhorted Timothy to "retain the standard of sound words which you have heard from me, in the faith and love that are in Christ Jesus" (2 Timothy 1:13). Doctrine is not an optional accessory to the Christian life—it is the foundation upon which one's faith is built. To reject or neglect doctrine is to remove the very structure that sustains spiritual life.

In contrast, false teachers promote what is "itching to the ears," offering novelty, mysticism, or moral compromise. They present teaching that appeals to emotions and human reasoning rather than divine revelation. True courage, therefore, begins with the unwavering conviction that Scripture alone—God-breathed and inerrant—is sufficient for all doctrine, correction, and training in righteousness (2 Timothy 3:16–17).

Remaining faithful requires continual study, meditation, and discernment. Believers must test every teaching by comparing it with the Word of God, as the Bereans did (Acts 17:11). Those who remain anchored in Scripture will not be easily "tossed about by every wind of teaching" (Ephesians 4:14).

Courage to Confront False Teaching

The courage to confront falsehood is an indispensable part of defending the faith. The apostle Paul did not hesitate to "rebuke sharply" those who contradicted sound teaching (Titus 1:13). True Christian love does not tolerate doctrinal deception; it exposes it. The believer must recognize that silence in the face of error is not humility—it is complicity.

Confronting false teaching requires both discernment and spiritual fortitude. Many today shrink from confrontation, fearing division or unpopularity. Yet, Paul warned Timothy, "Preach the word; be ready in season and out of season; reprove, rebuke, and exhort, with complete patience and teaching" (2 Timothy 4:2). Courage is not the absence of fear but the resolve to act rightly despite it. To stand for truth is to align with Jehovah, even if the majority stand against it.

False teachers often disguise themselves under the cloak of sincerity or eloquence. Paul wrote, "Such men are false apostles, deceitful workers, disguising themselves as apostles of Christ" (2 Corinthians 11:13). They mix truth with error, quoting Scripture but distorting its meaning. It requires courage to name error for what it is, especially when it comes from within one's own religious community. Yet, to protect the flock, such exposure is necessary. A shepherd who refuses to warn of wolves betrays his trust.

Courage also involves personal purity. One cannot confront error while harboring compromise. The one who stands against apostasy must himself be devoted to holiness, "keeping faith and a good conscience" (1 Timothy 1:19). The power to confront falsehood rests not merely in argument but in the authority of a life conformed to the truth.

Persevering When Many Turn Away

The believer's courage is tested most deeply when others fall away. When Jesus taught hard truths, "many of his disciples turned back and no longer walked with him" (John 6:66). The temptation to follow the crowd, to measure truth by numbers, has always been strong. Yet, the remnant who remain faithful understand that the path of life is narrow and few find it (Matthew 7:14).

Paul himself faced this loneliness: "At my first defense no one came to stand by me, but all deserted me" (2 Timothy 4:16). Still, he could say, "But the Lord stood by me and strengthened me." Perseverance amid apostasy requires that same assurance—that Christ is enough even when human companionship fails. The faithful must remember that spiritual decline around them does not alter the truth of God's Word.

Endurance also involves patience and hope. Apostasy will grow until Christ returns to judge the living and the dead, but those who hold fast to sound doctrine will receive the "crown of righteousness" (2 Timothy 4:8). The courage to endure is sustained by the certainty of Jehovah's promises. The believer does not persevere through human strength but through the empowering grace that comes from God.

Love for Truth Amid Deception

Love for truth is the essential mark that distinguishes genuine believers from apostates. Paul warned that those who perish "refused to love the truth and so be saved" (2 Thessalonians 2:10). It is not enough to know the truth intellectually; one must love it—embrace it, delight in it, and allow it to shape every aspect of life.

Apostasy flourishes where truth is treated as negotiable. Deception gains strength when emotions and experiences are placed above the authority of Scripture. The antidote is a deep affection for the Word of God, cultivated through continual meditation and obedience. David expressed this love beautifully: "Your word is a lamp to my feet and a light to my path" (Psalm 119:105).

Love for truth also manifests in a hatred of falsehood. Psalm 119:104 says, "Therefore I hate every false way." Genuine devotion to Christ leads believers to reject compromise with the world's philosophies and moral decay. To love the truth is to be loyal to the One who is "the way, and the truth, and the life" (John 14:6).

This love must be guarded, for deception in the last days will be powerful. Jesus warned that false Christs and false prophets will arise, performing signs and wonders to mislead, if possible, even the chosen ones (Mark 13:22). The believer's safeguard is continual immersion in the Word, reliance upon its wisdom, and the humility to be corrected by it.

Standing Alone if Necessary

True courage in the face of apostasy often means standing alone. Elijah thought he was the only prophet left who had not bowed to Baal (1 Kings 19:10). Jeremiah was mocked and imprisoned for proclaiming Jehovah's message. Daniel stood firm in a pagan empire. The pattern is clear: those who remain loyal to God's truth often find themselves isolated from the religious majority.

To stand alone for truth is not arrogance; it is obedience. The faithful do not measure success by popularity or acceptance, but by conformity to Scripture. When the majority abandon sound teaching, the remnant must remember that they are never truly alone. As Jehovah said to Elijah, "I have kept for myself seven thousand who have not bowed the knee to Baal" (Romans 11:4). God always preserves a faithful remnant who hold fast to His Word.

Standing alone also requires courage rooted in conviction, not emotion. Conviction comes from the settled assurance that Scripture is truth, that Christ reigns, and that eternal life belongs to those who persevere in obedience. The faithful must therefore speak truth even when it is unwelcome, live righteously even when it is ridiculed, and worship Jehovah even when others follow man-made traditions.

The believer who stands alone is sustained by the same promise given to Joshua: "Be strong and courageous. Do not be frightened, and do not be dismayed, for Jehovah your God is with you wherever you go" (Joshua 1:9). Courage is not self-confidence but God-confidence—the conviction that He will uphold those who remain steadfast in His truth.

Chapter 20 – The Triumph of the Fearless

Main Verse: *"He who overcomes will inherit these things, and I will be his God and he will be my son."* — Revelation 21:7

The Victory of the Faithful

The book of Revelation reveals not only the final judgment upon wickedness but also the glorious triumph of those who remain faithful to Jehovah through the most severe opposition. Revelation 21:7 declares, "He who overcomes will inherit these things, and I will be his God and he will be My son." This verse stands as both a promise and a reward — a divine assurance that perseverance in faith leads to eternal fellowship with God. The faithful are not described as those who merely survive; they are described as *overcomers*. Their victory is not by human might but through faith in Jesus Christ, the Son of God, who conquered sin and death through His sacrificial death and resurrection.

To "overcome" (Greek: *nikaō*) conveys the image of one who conquers through steadfast endurance. It is the same term used in Revelation 2 and 3 in Christ's messages to the congregations, where the overcomer receives promises of eternal reward: the right to eat from the tree of life, immunity from the second death, and entrance into the New Jerusalem. Thus, the overcomer is one who, through faith, obedience, and courage, continues in righteousness despite persecution, deception, or the allure of worldliness. The victory of the faithful is therefore not passive endurance but active conquest of evil through loyalty to Jehovah and Christ.

The victory of faith is seen most fully in the person of Jesus Christ. He overcame the world, as He declared in John 16:33: "In the world you have tribulation, but take courage; I have overcome the world." The faithful imitate this victory, not in divine power but in moral and spiritual steadfastness. They overcome sin, Satan, and the pressures of a corrupt system by maintaining integrity and trust in God's Word. Through faith, they resist temptation, endure persecution, and remain steadfast until the end.

The victory of the faithful also involves enduring the trials of this present world. Christians must resist fear and discouragement, for fear is the enemy of faith. The faithful recognize that fear paralyzes spiritual progress and hinders obedience. Jehovah repeatedly told His people throughout Scripture, "Do not be afraid," not because danger was absent, but because His presence was guaranteed. Faith transforms the weak into the courageous because it rests in the certainty of God's promises. Those who overcome do not rely on themselves but on the One who strengthens them.

The Eternal Reward of Courageous Endurance

Revelation 21:7 stands as a climactic promise — "He who overcomes will inherit these things." The context reveals what "these things" are: the new heaven and new earth, the New Jerusalem, and the eternal presence of God. These are not symbolic of abstract bliss but the real inheritance of those who remain faithful until the end. The inheritance includes eternal life, perfect fellowship with God, and participation in the restored creation free from sin, sorrow, and death.

Courageous endurance is central to the life of the believer. The endurance that leads to eternal reward is not a brief act of bravery but a lifelong commitment to righteousness and truth, even in the face of ridicule, loss, or persecution. Jesus said in Matthew 24:13, "The one who endures to the end, he will be saved." The endurance spoken of here is not simply surviving hardship but persevering in faith, resisting compromise, and holding firm to the Word of God.

The eternal reward is described as inheritance. This language recalls the ancient covenantal promise of inheritance given to Abraham, which was both physical and spiritual. In Christ, believers inherit the fulfillment of all divine promises. The inheritance is not earned by works but received by grace through faith. However, it is conditioned upon perseverance — not perfection, but persistence in faith and obedience.

Jehovah's declaration, "I will be his God and he will be My son," signifies complete reconciliation and intimate relationship. This fulfills the covenant formula repeated throughout Scripture, first expressed in Exodus 6:7 and later echoed in 2 Corinthians 6:16–18. The ultimate blessing of the redeemed is not merely eternal existence but restored relationship with God — the Father welcoming His children into eternal communion with Him.

Overcoming Through Faith

Faith is the instrument through which the believer overcomes. The apostle John wrote, "For whatever is born of God overcomes the world; and this is the victory that has overcome the world — our faith" (1 John 5:4). Faith is not wishful thinking or emotional optimism; it is confident trust in Jehovah and in His Son, Jesus Christ. Faith draws its strength from the reliability of God's Word and the reality of His promises.

Overcoming through faith involves rejecting the lies of the world, resisting the temptations of sin, and remaining loyal to Christ under pressure. The overcomer believes in God's truth even when the world promotes deceit. He stands firm on the Word of God even when human philosophies, false religions, and apostate teachings contradict it. His confidence is not in human reasoning but in divine revelation.

Faith not only enables endurance but transforms character. The one who overcomes does so because he trusts that Jehovah's promises are greater than the world's threats. The trials of faith refine the believer's character, producing steadfastness and maturity. As Peter wrote, "the proof of your faith, being more precious than gold which is perishable, even though tested by fire, may be found to result in praise and glory and honor at the revelation of Jesus Christ" (1 Peter 1:7). Through faith, the believer gains strength to endure what human courage alone cannot withstand.

The apostle Paul exemplified this overcoming faith. He endured imprisonment, persecution, and hardship yet declared, "I can do all things through Him who strengthens me" (Philippians 4:13). Faith transforms weakness into power, fear into confidence, and despair into hope. True faith never retreats in the face of adversity but advances, trusting that God's purposes will prevail.

Courage That Leads to Eternal Life

Courage in Scripture is not merely human boldness but spiritual fortitude rooted in trust in Jehovah. Joshua was commanded, "Be strong and courageous... for Jehovah your God is with you wherever you go" (Joshua 1:9). Courage flows from the awareness of divine presence and the certainty of divine promises. Without courage, faith remains theoretical; with courage, faith becomes active and victorious.

The courage that leads to eternal life is not reckless defiance but humble confidence in God's sovereignty. The fearless believer does not seek conflict but refuses to compromise truth for comfort. He stands firm when others yield, he confesses Christ when others remain silent, and he endures hardship for the sake of righteousness. Jesus said, "Do not fear those who kill the body but are unable to kill the soul; but rather fear Him who is able to destroy both soul and body in Gehenna" (Matthew 10:28). True courage is grounded in the fear of God, not in the fear of man.

Throughout Scripture, the faithful are characterized by their courage under pressure. Daniel faced the lions, not because he was fearless by nature, but because he feared disobedience to God more than death. The apostles preached boldly despite imprisonment and threats, knowing that obedience to God outweighed loyalty to men. Courage that leads to eternal life is sustained by faith, strengthened by prayer, and fueled by hope.

Revelation 21:8 presents a solemn contrast immediately following the promise to the overcomer: "But for the cowardly and unbelieving... their part will be in the lake that burns with fire and brimstone, which is the second death." Cowardice is listed first among the condemned, emphasizing that fear leading to unfaithfulness is spiritually fatal. The fearful are not those who experience natural emotion but those who allow fear to override obedience and faith. The triumph of the fearless lies in their unwavering commitment to truth regardless of opposition.

Edward D. Andrews

The Fearless Among the Redeemed

The redeemed are those who have been purchased by the blood of Christ and remain faithful to Him until the end. Among them are the fearless — those who conquer fear through faith. The fearless are not those who never feel fear, but those who refuse to yield to it. Their fear of Jehovah surpasses all other fears, producing reverence, obedience, and confidence.

In Revelation 14:4–5, the redeemed are described as those who "follow the Lamb wherever He goes" and "no lie was found in their mouth; they are blameless." This fearlessness flows from moral integrity and spiritual purity. The fearless among the redeemed are those who love truth, resist corruption, and stand apart from the world's immorality and deceit. Their courage stems from loyalty to Jehovah and Christ, not from pride or defiance.

Fearless faith is seen in the early Christians who faced persecution under Rome. Refusing to renounce Christ, they overcame the world's power through spiritual conviction. Their fearlessness was not born of strength but of assurance in the resurrection and eternal life. They believed Jesus' words: "Do not let your heart be troubled; believe in God, believe also in Me" (John 14:1). This kind of trust produces peace even in the midst of suffering.

The fearless are the spiritual heirs of all who have walked by faith — Abel, Noah, Abraham, Moses, and the prophets. Each faced opposition but remained steadfast. Their courage was not self-willed but divinely empowered through their trust in Jehovah. The fearless among the redeemed are those who follow this same pattern, living with eternal perspective and unshakable confidence in God's promises.

The Final Glory of the Overcomers

The destiny of the overcomers is the fulfillment of all divine promises. Revelation 21 describes the new creation — a renewed order free from death, mourning, crying, or pain. The overcomers inherit not merely an improved existence but eternal life in perfect harmony with Jehovah. They will dwell in His presence, for "the tabernacle of God is among men, and He will dwell among them" (Revelation 21:3). This final glory is the reward for those who remained fearless and faithful.

The final glory includes eternal intimacy with God. The phrase "I will be his God and he will be My son" reveals a relationship that transcends all earthly ties. This is the full realization of adoption as God's children, sharing in the blessings of divine fellowship forever. The overcomers' joy will not be in personal triumph but in the presence of their Redeemer.

The overcomers' triumph also marks the complete end of evil. Satan, sin, and death will be destroyed, never to threaten again. The righteous will shine in the light of God's glory, walking in perfect peace and righteousness. The overcomers' victory is everlasting because it is secured by the One who overcame death itself.

In this final glory, fear will be forever banished. Perfect love will reign, and the faithful will experience unbroken communion with Jehovah and the Lamb. The triumph of the fearless is therefore not only the conquest of fear in this life but the eternal enjoyment of peace in the life to come.

Appendix – Living Fearlessly in the Last Days

Main Verse: *"But the righteous will live by faith."* — Habakkuk 2:4

Understanding the Prophetic Warnings

The days in which we live are increasingly marked by spiritual apathy, moral degradation, global instability, and widespread deception. Yet none of this should come as a surprise to the faithful student of Scripture. Jehovah, in His unmatched wisdom, has provided ample prophetic warnings throughout His inspired Word. The purpose of biblical prophecy is not to incite fear or speculation but to instill vigilance and confidence in Jehovah's sovereignty. Habakkuk 2:4 serves as a timeless anchor in this regard: "But the righteous will live by faith." The context of this verse lies in the prophet's plea for understanding amidst national corruption and looming judgment. Jehovah's reply affirms that the arrogant will not endure, but those declared righteous through unwavering trust in God will survive and thrive spiritually.

Jesus Christ Himself issued detailed warnings about the time of the end. In Matthew 24, Mark 13, and Luke 21, He outlined the characteristics of the final days prior to His return: false messiahs, wars, famines, pestilences, earthquakes, increased lawlessness, and persecution of the holy ones. Paul reinforced these warnings in 2 Timothy 3:1–5, describing the last days as "difficult times" when people would be "lovers of themselves," "disloyal," and "lovers of pleasures rather than lovers of God." These prophecies are not abstract concepts but observable realities in today's global culture.

The book of Revelation, written by the apostle John around 96 C.E., expands on these themes with apocalyptic visions, unveiling the intensification of opposition to God's purposes, the rise of global political and religious deception, and the persecution of those loyal to Christ. The book's purpose is not to mystify, but to strengthen the resolve of the righteous, offering assurance that ultimate victory belongs to Jehovah and His Anointed One.

The Present Signs of the End Times

The moral, religious, and political climate of the modern world unmistakably mirrors the signs foretold by Jesus and the apostles. Globally, lawlessness has increased, and love has grown cold, fulfilling Matthew 24:12. The sanctity of life is undermined through rampant violence, the family structure is dismantled by immorality, and truth is suppressed by relativism. These are not isolated phenomena but the result of Satan's intensified activity, knowing that "he has a short period of time" (Revelation 12:12).

Religious deception abounds. False teachers promote a form of godliness but deny its power (2 Timothy 3:5), peddling a gospel of prosperity, tolerance of sin, and spiritual complacency. Entire denominations have abandoned biblical inerrancy, championing worldly philosophies in place of divine truth. The emergence of globalism and religious ecumenism has paved the way for the prophesied apostate religious system described as "Babylon the Great" in Revelation 17.

Politically, nations are in turmoil, marked by instability, shifting alliances, wars, and rumors of war (Matthew 24:6). These developments align precisely with the rise of the symbolic "wild beast" of Revelation 13, representing human governments under Satan's influence. Despite promises of peace and security, the world continues to spiral toward the climax foretold in 1 Thessalonians 5:3: "Whenever it is that they are saying, 'Peace and security!' then sudden destruction is to be instantly on them."

Edward D. Andrews

How to Remain Spiritually Awake

Jesus repeatedly exhorted His followers to remain awake and vigilant. In Matthew 24:42, He said, "Keep on the watch, therefore, because you do not know on what day your Lord is coming." To remain spiritually awake is to live with an acute awareness of the times, a devotion to prayer, and a daily commitment to God's Word.

Spiritual wakefulness demands constant discernment. The spiritually drowsy are easily led astray by material distractions, the cares of life, or by accommodating sin. But those who are awake actively seek Jehovah's will, examine themselves regularly, and hold firmly to the "accurate knowledge of the truth" (1 Timothy 2:4). Paul urged the believers in Thessalonica, "So, then, let us not sleep as the rest do, but let us stay awake and keep our senses" (1 Thessalonians 5:6). This includes staying rooted in daily Bible reading, association with fellow believers, and unceasing prayer.

Furthermore, vigilance is not passive. It is the resolve to keep oneself morally clean, doctrinally sound, and spiritually ready for Christ's return. As Jesus warned in the parable of the ten virgins (Matthew 25:1–13), only those who prepared in advance were welcomed into the marriage feast. The others, though claiming to wait for the bridegroom, were found lacking.

Guarding Against Deception and Apathy

Deception is the chief strategy of Satan, "the god of this system of things" (2 Corinthians 4:4), who blinds the minds of unbelievers and seeks to mislead even the chosen ones (Matthew 24:24). In the last days, this deception has reached unprecedented levels. It appears in religious garb, political ideologies, social movements, and even in so-called Christian pulpits.

Guarding against deception requires total allegiance to Scripture. All beliefs, teachings, and practices must be examined in the light of God's inspired Word (Acts 17:11). Emotionalism, tradition, or consensus cannot replace the authority of the Bible. As 2 Timothy 3:16–17 affirms, "All Scripture is inspired by God and beneficial for teaching, for reproving, for setting things straight, for disciplining in righteousness, so that the man of God may be fully competent, completely equipped for every good work."

Apathy, on the other hand, is spiritual paralysis. Jesus condemned the lukewarm condition of the Laodicean congregation in Revelation 3:15–16. Today, many professing Christians exhibit this same lukewarmness, attending services out of habit, possessing Bibles they rarely read, and offering prayers devoid of zeal or faith. The call is clear: "Become zealous and repent" (Revelation 3:19). Fearlessness in the last days comes not from emotional confidence but from the conviction born of spiritual sobriety and diligence.

Edward D. Andrews

Building Faith That Endures the Final Test

Faith is not merely an initial response to the gospel but the sustaining power that carries the believer through every hardship. Habakkuk 2:4, quoted repeatedly in the New Testament (Romans 1:17; Galatians 3:11; Hebrews 10:38), underscores that the righteous live continually by faith. This faith must be nurtured and guarded, as Jesus emphasized in Luke 18:8, "When the Son of man comes, will he really find this faith on the earth?"

Enduring faith is built through consistent engagement with God's Word. Romans 10:17 states, "So faith comes from hearing, and hearing through the word about Christ." The believer who feeds on Scripture, obeys its commands, and prays in harmony with it, will find strength to stand amid the pressures of the last days.

Trials, opposition, and temptations will intensify. But those who trust in Jehovah will not be shaken. Faith rests not in feelings or outcomes but in the character and promises of God. As Hebrews 11 outlines, men and women of old endured persecution, exile, and death, looking forward to "a better resurrection" (Hebrews 11:35). Their example urges us to "run with endurance the race that is set before us" (Hebrews 12:1), fixing our eyes on Jesus, the "Perfecter of our faith."

Looking Forward to the Return of Christ

The return of Jesus Christ is not a vague hope but a guaranteed reality firmly established by Scripture. Acts 1:11 records the angelic promise at His ascension: "This Jesus who has been taken up from you into heaven will come in the same manner as you have seen him going into heaven." His return will be visible, personal, and powerful—ushering in judgment on the ungodly and reward for the faithful.

The New Testament writers consistently emphasized the return of Christ as the believer's hope and motivation. Paul wrote in Titus 2:13, "while we wait for the happy hope and glorious manifestation of the great God and of our Savior, Jesus Christ." This hope energizes holiness, motivates endurance, and instills courage in the face of opposition.

This return, however, will not bring joy to all. For the unrepentant, it will be a day of wrath and destruction (2 Thessalonians 1:7–9). The current delay is not due to divine forgetfulness but divine mercy. As 2 Peter 3:9 explains, "Jehovah is not slow concerning his promise… but he is patient with you because he does not desire anyone to be destroyed but desires all to attain to repentance."

Those who live fearlessly in the last days do so not by ignoring the reality of coming judgment but by living in preparation for it. Their lives are marked by purity, zeal, and steadfastness. They anticipate the moment when "the Son of man comes in His glory" (Matthew 25:31), ready to be found faithful.

The final days are not something for Christians to dread, but to confront with boldness and hope. Those who live by faith—an obedient, enduring, truth-centered faith—will not shrink back but will stand approved, ready to inherit the promises.

Bibliography

Andrews, E. (2018). *THE EARLY CHRISTIAN COPYISTS OF THE NEW TESTAMENT: The Making and Copying of the New Testament Books.* Cambridge: Christian Publishing House.

Andrews, E. (2020). *FROM SPOKEN WORDS TO SACRED TEXTS: Introduction-Intermediate New Testament Textual Studies.* Cambridge: Christian Publishing House.

Andrews, E. D. (2011). *AN INTRODUCTION TO BIBLE DIFFICULTIES So-Called Errors and Contradictions.* Cambridge: Christian Publishing House.

Andrews, E. D. (2012). *DIFFICULTIES IN THE BIBLE UPDATED: Updated and Expanded.* Cambridge, OH: Christian Publishing House.

Andrews, E. D. (2015). *CRISIS OF FAITH: Saving Those Who Doubt .* Cambridge, OH: Christian Publishing House.

Andrews, E. D. (2016). *HOMOSEXUALITY - THE BIBLE AND THE CHRISTIAN: Basic Bible Doctrines of the Christian Faith.* Cambridge, OH: Christian Publishing House.

Andrews, E. D. (2016). *INTERPRETING THE BIBLE: Introduction to Biblical Hermeneutics.* Cambridge, OH: Christian Publishing House.

Andrews, E. D. (2016). *THE BATTLE FOR THE CHRISTIAN MIND: Be Transformed by the Renewal of Your Mind.* Cambridge, OH: Christian Publishing House.

Andrews, E. D. (2016). *THE CHRISTIAN APOLOGIST: Always Being Prepared to Make a Defense [Second Edition].* Cambridge, OH: Christian Publishing House.

Andrews, E. D. (2016). *THE COMPLETE GUIDE to BIBLE TRANSLATION: Bible Translation Choices and Translation Principles [Second Edition]*. Cambridge: Christian Publishing House.

Andrews, E. D. (2016). *THE EVANGELISM HANDBOOK: How All Christians Can Effectively Share God's Word in Their Community, [SECOND EDITION].* Cambridge, OH: Christian Publishing House.

Andrews, E. D. (2017). *CONVERSATIONAL EVANGELISM: Defending the Faith, Reasoning from the Scriptures, Explaining and Proving, Instructing in Sound Doctrine, and Overturning False Reasoning [Second Edition].* Cambridge, OH: Christian Publishing House.

Andrews, E. D. (2017). *DEFENDING OLD TESTAMENT AUTHORSHIP: The Word of God Is Authentic and True.* Cambridge, OH: Christian Publishing House.

Andrews, E. D. (2017). *EARLY CHRISTIANITY IN THE FIRST CENTURY: Jesus' Witnesses to the Ends of the Earth.* Cambridge, OH: Christian Publishing House.

Andrews, E. D. (2017). *HOW TO STUDY YOUR BIBLE: Rightly Handling the Word of God.* Cambridge, OH: Christian Publishing House.

Andrews, E. D. (2017). *IS THE QURAN THE WORD OF GOD?: Is Islam the One True Faith.* Cambridge, OH: Christian Publishing House.

Andrews, E. D. (2018). *CHRISTIAN APOLOGETIC EVANGELISM: Reaching Hearts with the Art of Persuasion.* Cambridge, OH: Christian Publishing House.

Andrews, E. D. (2018). *REASONING FROM THE SCRIPTURES: Sharing CHRIST as You Help Others to Learn about the Mighty works of God.* Cambridge, Ohio: Christian Publishing House.

Andrews, E. D. (2018). *REASONING WITH THE WORLD'S VARIOUS RELIGIONS: Examining and Evangelizing Other Faiths.* Cambridge, OH: Christian Publishing House.

Andrews, E. D. (2018). *The CHURCH CURE: Overcoming Church Problems.* Cambridge, OH: Christian Publishing House.

Andrews, E. D. (2019). *MIRACLES: What Does the Bible Really Teach?* Cambridge, OH: Christian Publishing House.

Andrews, E. D. (2019). *THE READING CULTURE OF EARLY CHRISTIANITY: The Production, Publication, Circulation, and Use of Books in the Early Christian Church.* Cambridge, OH: Christian Publishing House.

Andrews, E. D. (2020). *INERRANCY OF SCRIPTURE: How Can We Believe Inerrancy of Scripture In the Originals When We Don't Have the Originals?* Cambridge, OH: Christian Publishing House.

Andrews, E. D. (2022). *THE QUEST FOR THE HISTORICAL JESUS: Are Doubts About Jesus Justified?* Cambridge, OH: Christian Publishing House.

Andrews, E. D. (2023). *ARCHAEOLOGY & THE NEW TESTAMENT.* Cambridge, Ohio: Christian publishing House.

Andrews, E. D. (2023). *ARCHAEOLOGY & THE OLD TESTAMENT.* Cambridge, Ohio: Christian Publishing House.

Andrews, E. D. (2023). *BIBLICAL EXEGESIS: Biblical Criticism on Trial.* Cambridge, OH: Christian Publishing House.

Andrews, E. D. (2023). *CHRISTIAN APOLOGETICS: Answering the Tough Questions: Evidence and Reason in Defense of the Faith.* Cambridge, Ohio: Christian Publishing House.

Andrews, E. D. (2023). *HOW WE GOT THE BIBLE.* Cambridge, OH: Christian Publishing House.

Andrews, E. D. (2023). *ISLAM & THE QURAN: Examining the Quran & Islamic Teachings.* Cambridge, OH: Christian Publishing House.

Andrews, E. D. (2023). *ISLAMIC ESCHATOLOGY: Awaiting Al-Mahdi—The Twelfth Imam and the Future of Islam.* Cambridge, OH: Christian Publishing House.

Andrews, E. D. (2023). *JOHN CALVIN: A Solitary Quest for the Truth.* Cambridge, Ohio: Christian Publishing House.

Andrews, E. D. (2023). *THE BIBLE ON TRIAL: Examining the Evidence for Being Inspired, Inerrant, Authentic, and True.* Cambridge, Ohio: Christian Publishing House.

Andrews, E. D. (2023). *THE MACCABEES: The Hasmonaean Dynasty between Malachi and Matthew.* Cambridge, OH: Christian Publishing House.

Andrews, E. D. (2024). *BATTLE PLANS: A Game Plan for Answering Objections to the Christian Faith.* Cambridge, OH: Christian Publishing House.

Andrews, E. D. (2024). *CHRISTIAN APOLOGISTS OF THE SECOND CENTURY: Christian Defenders of the Faith.* Cambridge, OH: Christian Publishing House.

Andrews, E. D. (2024). *CHRISTIAN THEOLOGY: The Christian's Ultimate Guide to Learning from the Bible.* Cambridge, OH: Christian Publishing House.

Andrews, E. D. (2024). *CREATION AND COSMOS: A Journey Through Creation, Science, and the Origins of Life.* Cambridge, OH: Christian Publishing House.

Andrews, E. D. (2024). *DO WE STILL NEED A LITERAL BIBLE?: Discover the Truth about Literal Bibles.* Cambridge, OH: Christian Publishing House.

Andrews, E. D. (2024). *FAITH UNDER FIRE: Refuting the Top 30 Arguments Atheists Make Against Christianity.* Cambridge, OH: Christian Publishing House.

Andrews, E. D. (2024). *HELL: All You Need to Know About Hell.* Cambridge, OH: Christian Publishing House.

Andrews, E. D. (2024). *REASON MEETS FAITH: Addressing and Refuting Atheism's Challenges to Christianity.* Cambridge, OH: Christian Publishing House.

Andrews, E. D. (2024). *THE BABYLONIAN EMPIRE.* Cambridge, OH: Christian Publishing House.

Andrews, E. D. (2024). *THE BATTLE OF JERICHO—Myth or Fact?* Cambridge, OH: Christian Publishing House.

Andrews, E. D. (2024). *THE ENCYCLOPEDIA OF CHRISTIAN APOLOGETICS: The Resource for*

Pastors, Teachers, and Believers. Cambridge: Christan Publishing House.

Andrews, E. D. (2024). *THE HISTORICAL ADAM & EVE: Reconciling Faith and Fact in Genesis.* Cambridge, OH: Christian Publishing House.

Andrews, E. D. (2024). *THE HISTORICAL JESUS: The Death, Burial, and Resurrection of Jesus Christ.* Cambridge, OH: Christian Publishing House.

Andrews, E. D. (2024). *UNDERSTANDING THE HITTITES: Biblical History, Archaeological Discoveries, and Etymological Clarifications.* Cambridge, OH: Christian Publishing House.

Andrews, E. D. (2025). *A FRESH LOOK AT PAUL'S THEOLOGY: Biblical Theology as Revealed through Paul.* Cambridge, OH: Christian Publishing House.

Andrews, E. D. (2025). *ATHEISM: What Will You Say to an Atheist.* Cambridge, OH: Christian Publising House.

Andrews, E. D. (2025). *BIBLE DIFFICULTIES: How to Approach Difficulties In the Bible.* Cambridge, OH: Christian Publishing House.

Andrews, E. D. (2025). *BIBLICAL WORDS AND THEIR MEANING: An Introduction to Lexical Semantics.* Cambridge, OH: Christian Publishing House.

Andrews, E. D. (2025). *CAN WE TRUST THE BIBLE?* Cambridge, OH: Christian Publishing House.

Andrews, E. D. (2025). *DISCOVERING GENESIS ANSWERS: Exploring the Historical and Cultural Contexts of Genesis, One Insight at a Time (Answers from Genesis).* Cambridge, OH: Christian Publishing House.

Andrews, E. D. (2025). *DISCOVERING GENESIS ANSWERS: Tackling Tough Questions in Genesis: One Solution at a Time (Answers from Genesis).* Cambridge, OH: Christian Publishing House.

Andrews, E. D. (2025). *DISCOVERING GENESIS ANSWERS: Unveiling the Truths of Creation, One Answer at a Time (Answers from Genesis).* Cambridge, OH: Chritian Publishing House.

Andrews, E. D. (2025). *EARLY CHRISTIANITY: Exploring Backgrounds, Historical Settings, and Cultures.* Cambridge, OH: Christian Publishing House.

Andrews, E. D. (2025). *IMMORTALITY OF THE SOUL: The Birth of the Doctrine.* Cambridge, OH: Christian Publishing Hiuse.

Andrews, E. D. (2025). *ISLAMIC IDEOLOGICAL JIHAD: Islamic-Funded, Islamic-Indoctrinated, Western Youth.* Cambridge, OH: Christian Publishing House.

Andrews, E. D. (2025). *JOSEPHUS & THE NEW TESTAMENT: Evidence from the First-Century Jewish Historian on Key Biblical Figures, Groups, and Events.* Cambridge, OH: Christian Publishng House.

Andrews, E. D. (2025). *LINGUISTICS AND THE BIBLICAL TEXT: Unlocking Scripture Through the Science of Language.* Cambridge, OH: Christian Publishing House.

Andrews, E. D. (2025). *OVERCOMING BIBLE DIFFICULTIES: Answers to the So-Called Errors and Contradictions [Second Edition].* Cambridge: Christian Publishing House.

Andrews, E. D. (2025). *PROVING GOD'S EXISTENCE.* Cambridge, OH: Christian Publishing House.

Andrews, E. D. (2025). *THE ANDREWS BIBLE BLUEPRINT: Unlocking Scripture's Truth, History, and Wisdom.* Cambridge, OH: Christian Publishing House.

Andrews, E. D. (2025). *THE ENCYCLOPEDIA OF THE TEXT OF THE NEW TESTAMENT: The Resource for Pastors, Teachers, and Believers.* Cambridge, OH: Christian Publishing House.

Andrews, E. D. (2025). *THE FACES OF ISLAM: Faith or Facade: Decoding Islam's Strategies.* Cambridge, OH: Christian Publishing House.

Andrews, E. D. (2025). *THE GUIDE TO SPIRITUAL WARFARE: Standing Firm in the Armor of God Against the Schemes of the Devil.* Cambridge, OH: Christian Publishing House.

Andrews, E. D. (2025). *THE STONES SPEAK: Biblical Archaeology and the Reliability of the Bible.* Cambridge, OH: Christian Publishing House.

Andrews, E. D. (2025). *WONDERFULLY MADE: Wonderful Are God's Works.* Cambridge, OH: Christian Publishing House.

Andrews, E. D. (2025). *YOUR YOUTH: The Young Christian's Guide to Making Right Choices.* Cambridge, OH: Christian Pubishing House.

Beattie, F. (2022). *CHRISTIAN APOLOGETICS [Annotated]: The Rational Vindication of Christianity.* Cambridge, OH: Christian Publishing House.

Kephart, E. B. (2022). *APOLOGETICS Annotated: A Treatise on Christian Evidences - [Annotated].* Cambridge, OH: Christian Publishing House.

www.ingramcontent.com/pod-product-compliance
Lightning Source LLC
LaVergne TN
LVHW020929090426
835512LV00020B/3279